MW01029701

PROBLEMS
OF
HUMANITY

by

ALICE A. BAILEY

LUCIS PUBLISHING COMPANY
New York

LUCIS PRESS LTD.
London

First Edition 1947
Third and Revised Edition 1964
Seventh Printing 1993

ISBN 0-85330-113-1
Library of Congress Catalog Card Number: 53-2808

The publication of this book is financed by the Tibetan Book
Fund which is established for the perpetuation of the teachings of
the Tibetan and Alice A. Bailey.

This fund is controlled by the Lucis Trust, a tax-exempt,
religious, educational corporation.

The Lucis Publishing Company is a non-profit organisation
owned by the Lucis Trust. No royalties are paid on this book.

*This title has been translated into Dutch, Spanish, French, Italian,
German and Greek. Translation into other languages is proceeding.*

LUCIS PUBLISHING COMPANY
113 University Place, 11th Fl.
P.O. Box 722, Cooper Station
New York, NY 10276

LUCIS PRESS, LTD.
Suite 54
3 Whitehall Court
London SW1A 2EF

MANUFACTURED IN THE UNITED STATES OF AMERICA
BY THE FORT ORANGE PRESS, INC., ALBANY, N.Y.

FOREWORD

The first edition of this book, published in 1947, contained essays on the basic problems of humanity. These had originally been issued in pamphlet form between October 1944 and December 1946, and dealt essentially with conditions during and immediately after the War years of 1939–45.

In 1953 a second edition was published which omitted outdated material. A further revision was made for the third edition in 1964. Since then, the progress made by humanity has been such that the nature of the problems has changed to a marked degree. For example, problems relating to the world's children continue to exist but in different forms and under different conditions to those of the post–War period. The problems of capital, labour and employment have changed greatly in an increasingly automated and computerised world. Significant developments within the many branches of orthodox religion are presenting new problems within the world's faiths.

Similar comments can be made on all the problems considered. In addition, new problems are arising under present day conditions, although these can usefully be viewed as variations and extensions of the basic six problems discussed in this book.

So now, in 1993, when we need to reprint the book again, we have had to consider whether it would be better to cut the original text to the bone and graft onto the skeletal structure factual data and information supplied by other writers, or whether we should reprint the book as it stands. Because the basic teaching on all the problems is still as sound, as dynamic and as necessary as it was when originally written, we have decided to do the latter.

But it is important that those who study this book are aware of its history so that the essential teaching can be recognised and absorbed and the irrelevant factors ignored. The spiritual principles to be applied to the problems of humanity as discussed in this book are valid today and remain largely ignored by the majority of humanity. The contribution of esoteric students in creating "the thoughtform of solution" to human problems in a world at crisis point is a vital and practical service.

Problems of Humanity Study Course

A study course on the Problems of Humanity is offered by World Goodwill. Based on the insights of this book, the course is regularly updated and presents a spiritual and contemporary view of world problems.

Write to the publishers for further information.

LUCIS PUBLISHING COMPANY, New York, London—1993

TABLE OF CONTENTS

INTRODUCTION

It is essential that all thinking people should give time and thought to the consideration of the major world problems with which we are now faced. Some of them can be solved with relative rapidity—given common sense and a correctly appreciated self-interest; others will require foresighted planning and a long patience as, one by one, the necessary steps are taken, leading to the readjustment of human values and the inauguration of new attitudes of mind regarding right human relations. In the recognition of the growth in human consciousness and in a realization of the distinction obviously existing between primitive men and our modern intelligent humanity lie the grounds for an unshaken optimism as to human destiny.

Events in the immediate foreground do not blot out the long history of human development and obliterate recognition of the long range changes which have taken place within the human consciousness; these basically condition human objectives, all human contacts and underline with understanding and perspective the reactions of the race of men.

The slow and restricted movements of the primitive races of mankind have given place to the speed and the rapid movement (the almost unbelievably rapid movement) and transportation facilities of the airplane. The uncouth sounds and the limited vocabulary of the savage races have developed into the intricate language systems of the present nations; the various modes of primitive communication by means of drums or bonfires have been replaced by the telegraph, the telephone and the radio; the wooden dug-out of the uncultured islanders has developed into the greyhound of the sea, racing from port to port under mechanical power and in the space of a few short days; the early slow modes of travel by foot, on horseback or by chariot have given way to the trains, speeding across entire continents at the rate of seventy miles an hour or more. The early and simple civilizations have been succeeded by the intricate and highly organized social, economic and political civilization of modern times. The culture of the ages, the arts, literature, the music and the philosophy of all time is today at the disposal of the average citizen.

The above contrasts provide a perspective and a background which will inspire hope for the future and confidence in the ultimate destiny of man. The past is in reality more like the prenatal stage than an ordinary living process; it is a preface to a richer and a more enlightened life; it is a preliminary period to a culture and a civilization which will redound to the glory of God and constitute a vital testimony to the divinity of man.

When the birthing process is over, a new humanity will be seen active upon the earth, a new race of men— new because differently oriented.

There are necessarily many lesser problems but those dealt with in this book cover the major ones with which humanity is at this time confronted, and which must find some solution during the next twenty-five years. This will have to be done by the simple method (simple to write but difficult to implement) of *establishing right human relations between men and between nations*.

The immediate spiritual problem with which all are faced is the problem of gradually offsetting hate and initiating the new technique of trained, imaginative, creative and practical goodwill.

Goodwill is man's first attempt to express the love of God. Its results on earth will be peace. It is so simple and practical that people fail to appreciate its potency or its scientific and dynamic effect. One person sincerely practicing goodwill in a family can completely change its attitudes. Goodwill really practiced among groups in any nation, by political and religious parties in any nation and among the nations of the world can revolutionize the world.

The key to humanity's trouble (focussing as it has in the economic difficulties of the past two hundred years and in the theological impasse of the orthodox churches) has been to take and not give, to accept and not share, to grasp and not to distribute. This has involved the breaking of a law which has placed humanity in a position of positive guilt. War is the dire penalty which mankind has had to pay for this great sin of separateness. Impressions from the Hierarchy have been received, distorted, misapplied and misinterpreted and the task of the New Group of World Servers is to offset this evil.

Humanity has never really lived up to the teaching given it. Spiritual impression, whether conveyed by the Christ, by Krishna or by Buddha (and passed on to the masses by Their disciples) has not yet been expressed as it was hoped. Men do not live up to what they already know; they fail to make practical their information; they short circuit the light; they do not discipline themselves; greedy desire and unlawful ambition control and not the inner knowledge. To put it scientifically and from the esoteric angle: Spiritual impression has been interrupted and there has been interference with the divine circulatory flow. It is the task of the disciples of the world to restore this flow and to stop this interference. This is the major problem facing spiritual people at this time.

CHAPTER I

THE PSYCHOLOGICAL REHABILITATION
OF THE NATIONS

THIS problem is far more complicated and deep-seated than might appear at the first glance. Had we only to deal with the national psychoses and the mental conditions induced by the act of war and participation in it, the problem would be acute enough but it could be solved easily by the restitution of security, by the sound psychological treatment of the differing nationalities, by their physical rehabilitation and by the restoration of liberty, opportunity, leisure and, above all, by the organization of the men and women of goodwill. This latter group would show themselves as willing to carry forward the needed educational processes and (which is far more important) they would endeavor to convey spiritual inspiration—something which humanity sorely needs at this time. There are enough men and women of goodwill in the world today to accomplish this *if* they can be reached, inspired and supported in their endeavor, both materially and spiritually.

The situation is far more difficult than a casual analysis would make it seem. The psychological problem involved has a background which is centuries old, which is inherent in the soul of each individual nation and which is potently conditioning the minds of all their peoples today. It is here that our major difficulty lies and it is one which will not easily give way to any effort or to any spiritual endeavor, whether carried out by the organized churches (which show a woeful lack of appreciation of the problem) or by spiritually minded groups and individuals.

The work to be done is so acutely needed and the perils of its non-accomplishment are so appalling that it is necessary to indicate certain major lines of danger and certain national aptitudes which carry a menace to the peace of the world. These problems fall naturally into two categories:

I. The internal, psychological problems of the individual nations.

II. Major world problems, such as the relation between nations and business and the forces of labor.

Before the world can be a safer, sweeter, saner and more beautiful place, all the nations must take stock of themselves and begin to handle their own psychological weaknesses and complexes. Each nation must aim at sound mental health and endeavor to implement sound, psychological objectives. International unity must be attained and this should be based not only upon mutual trust but also upon correct world objectives and true psychological understanding.

Men and women everywhere are already striving towards individual betterment; groups in every nation are similarly motivated; the urge to move forward into greater beauty of expression, of character and of living conditions is the outstanding eternal characteristic of mankind. In the earlier stages of racial history, this urge showed itself in a desire for better material circumstances and surroundings; today, this urge expresses itself in a demand for beauty, leisure and culture; it voices the opportunity to work creatively and passes gradually but inevitably into the stage where right human relations become of prime importance.

Today a great and unique opportunity faces every nation. Hitherto the problem of psychological integration, of intelligent living, of spiritual growth and of divine revelation has been approached solely from the angle of man, the unit. Owing to the scientific achievements of mankind (as a result of the unfolding human intellect), it is now possible to think in far wider terms and to see humanity in a truer perspective. Our horizon is extending into infinity; our eyes are no longer focussed upon our immediate foreground. The family unit is now recognized in relation to the community, and the community is seen as an integral and effective part of the city, state or nation. Dimly, and as yet ineffectually, we are projecting this same concept into the field of international relations. Thinkers throughout the world are functioning internationally; this is the guarantee of the future because only when men can think in these wider terms will the fusion of all men everywhere become possible, will brotherhood come into being and *humanity* be a fact in our consciousness.

Most men today think in terms of their own nation or group and this is their largest concept; they have progressed beyond the stage of their individual physical and mental well-being and are visioning the possibility of adding their quota of usefulness and of stability to the national whole; they are seeking to be cooperative, to understand and to further the good of the community. This is not rare but is descriptive of many thousands in every nation. This spirit and attitude will some day characterize the attitude of nation to nation. At present this is *not* so, and a very different psychology rules. Nations seek and demand the best for themselves, no matter what the cost to others; they regard this as a right attitude and as characteristic of good citizenship. Nations are colored by hatreds and prejudices, many of which are as unwarranted today as foul language in a religious meeting. Nations are split and divided within themselves by racial barriers, by party differences and by religious attitudes. These inevitably bring disorder and finally disaster.

An intense spirit of nationalism—assertive and boastful—distinguishes the citizens of most countries, particularly in relation to each other. This breeds dislike, distrust and the disruption of right human relations. All nations are guilty of these qualities and attitudes, expressed according to their individual culture and genius. All nations, as all families, have also in them groups or individuals who are recognized sources of trouble to the well-intentioned remainder. There are nations within the international community which are and have been for a long time disrupting agencies.

The problem of the interplay and interaction of the nations is largely a psychological one. The soul of a nation is potent in its effect. The national thoughtform (built up over the centuries by the thinking, the goals and the ambitions of a nation) constitutes its ideal objective and is most effective in conditioning the people. A Pole, a Frenchman, an American, a Hindu, a Britisher or a German are easily recognized, no matter where they may be. This recognition is not based solely upon appearance, intonation or habits but primarily upon the expressed mental attitude, the sense of relativity and a general national assertiveness. These indications express reaction to the particular national thoughtform under which the man has been raised. If this reaction makes him a good cooperative citizen within the national boundaries, that is good and to be desired. If it makes him assertive, arrogant, critical of the nationals of other countries and separative in his thinking, he is then contributing to world disunity and, en masse, to international disruption. This menaces the peace of the world. The problem, therefore, becomes one in which all people share. Nations can be (and often are) anti-social, and all nations have within them these anti-social elements.

Self-interest distinguishes most men at this time, with attendant weaknesses. Yet, in all countries, there are those who have outgrown these self-centered attitudes and there are many who are more interested in civic and the national good than in themselves. A few, a very few in relation to the mass of men, are internationally minded and preoccupied with the welfare of humanity, as a whole. They eagerly desire recognition of the one world, of the one humanity.

The stage of national selfishness and the fixed determination to preserve national integrity—interpreted often in terms of boundaries and the expansion of trade —must gradually fade out. The nations must pass eventually to a more beneficent realization and come to the point where they regard their national cultures, their national resources and their ability to serve mankind as the contributions which they must make to the good of the whole. Emphasis upon worldly possessions or extensive territory is no sign of maturity; fighting to preserve these or to expand them is a sign of adolescent immaturity. Mankind is now growing up; only now is humanity demonstrating a wider sense of responsibility, of ability to handle its problems or to think in larger terms. The late world war was symptomatic of immaturity, of adolescent thinking, of uncontrolled childish emotions and of a demand—by anti-social nations—for that which does not belong to them. Like children, they cry for "more".

The intense isolationism and the "hands off" policy of certain groups in the United States, the demand for a white Australia or South Africa, the cry of "America for the Americans", or British Imperialism, the shouting of France for recognition, are other instances. They all indicate inability to think in larger terms; they are an expression of world irresponsibility; they indicate also the childishness of the race which fails to grasp the extent of the whole of which each nation is a part. War and the constant demand for territorial boundaries, based on ancient history, the holding on to material, national possessions at the expense of other people will seem some day to a more mature race of men like nursery quarrels over some favorite toy. The challenging cry of "This is *mine*" will some day no longer be heard.   In the meantime, this aggressive, immature spirit culminated in the war of 1914-1945. A thousand years hence, history will regard this as the acme of childish selfishness, started by grasping children who could not be stopped in their aggressive ways because the other nations were still too childish to take strong action when the first indications of the war were seen.

The race faces a new crisis of opportunity wherein new values can be seen as important, wherein the establishing of right human relations will be deemed desirable, not only from the idealistic point of view but also from the purely selfish angle.   Some day the principles of cooperation and of sharing will be substituted for those of possessive greed and competition. This is the inevitable next step ahead for humanity— one for which the entire evolutionary process has prepared mankind.

It was selfishness and self-interest which prevented several nations from siding with the Forces of Light; they preserved a selfish neutrality and lengthened the war by years. Is it not possible that when Germany first marched into Poland and when France and Great Britain consequently declared war upon Germany, if the entire civilized world of nations (without exception) had likewise declared war and banded together for the defeat of the aggressor, the war would not have lasted as long as it did? Interior politics, international jealousies, ancient distrusts and hatreds, fear and a refusal to recognize the facts produced disunity. Had all nations seen clearly and renounced their individual selfishness in 1939, the war would have been over much earlier. Had all the nations swung into action when Japan first went into Manchuria or Italy into Ethiopia, the war which has devastated the entire planet would not have been possible. To that extent, there is no nation without blame.

It is needful to make this clear so that there may be straight thinking as we face the world of today and begin to take the steps which will, in due course of time, lead to world security. This period should be faced by every nation with a sense of individual guilt and of innate psychological failure. It is hard to admit that none of the nations (including our own) has clean hands, and that all are guilty of greed and theft, of separativeness, of pride and prejudice, as well as national and racial hatreds. All nations have much interior housecleaning to do and this they must carry forward along with their outer efforts to bring about a better and more habitable world. It must be a world consciousness, motivated by the idea of the general good, one in which higher values than individual and national gain are emphasized and one in which people are trained in right national citizenship upon the one hand and on the other in the responsibility for world citizenship.

Is this too idealistic a picture? The guarantee of its possibility lies in the fact that thousands today are thinking along these idealistic lines; thousands are occupied with planning a better world and thousands are talking about the possibility. All ideas which emanate from the divine in man and nature eventually become ideals (even though somewhat distorted in the process) and these ideals finally become the governing principles of the masses. This is the true sequence of the historical process.

It might be of value to study briefly some of the psychological adjustments which the nations must make within their own borders, because reform begins at home. Then let us look at the world picture and gain a new vision. There is a scientific basis for the old statement in the Bible that "where there is no vision, the people perish".

History indicates a long past of battle, of war, of changing frontiers, of the discovery and prompt annexation of new territory, involving the subjugation of the original inhabitants, sometimes greatly to their benefit but always inexcusable. The spirit of nationalism and its growth is the background of modern history as taught in our schools, feeding national pride, engendering national enmities, racial hatreds and jealousies. History concerns itself with the lines of demarcation between countries and with the type of rule each country developed. These lines of demarcation are fiercely held and passports, as instituted this century, indicate the crystallization of the idea. History portrays the fierce determination of every nation to preserve its boundaries at any cost, to keep its culture and civilization intact, to add to them when possible and to share nothing with any other nation except for commercial profit, for which international legislation is provided. Yet all the time humanity is one humanity and the products of the earth belong to all. This wrong attitude has not only fostered the sense of separateness but has led to the exploitation of the weaker groups by the stronger and the wrecking of the economic life of the masses by a mere handful of powerful groups.

Ancient habits of mass thinking and of mass reaction are difficult to overcome. It is here that the main battleground of the world is found. Public opinion will have to be re-educated. The nations are reverting to the deep-seated modes of behavior and thought which have characterized them for generations. We need, in the general interest, to face up to our past, to recognize the new trends, to renounce the old ways of thinking and acting if humanity is not to descend to greater depths than in the last war.

The voices of the old order and the demand of the reactionary elements can be heard in every country, plus the demands of certain radical groups. Because they have been so long established, the voices of the conservatives carry weight and because humanity is tired, almost any action will be taken to ensure a rapid return to the normalcy, demanded by the conservatives, *unless* those who have the new vision act with promptness and with wisdom—and of this there is too little indication at this time.

FRANCE

A clamor is arising from France that her ancient glory be recognized, that her ancient task of representing the major, civilizing influence in old Europe be remembered, and that France be safeguarded and protected. She demands that nothing be done without consulting her. Yet for decades, France has given to the world a picture of great disunity and of political corruption and graft; she has always evidenced a deep love and desire for material gratification, priding herself on her realism, but not on any spiritual idealism, and substituting the brilliance of the intellect and keen scientific perception for the subjective realities. Has France learned from her collapse in the summer of 1940 that the values of the spirit must take the place of those which have hitherto motivated her? Does she realize that she has to regain the respect of the world—a respect which she lost when she surrendered and sought collaboration, thus proving herself innately weaker than those much smaller nations which fought until forced to accept defeat? Can France emerge from this time of trial, purified and able to demonstrate a new capacity to think in terms of unselfish international relations and not solely in terms of the material civilization which she demonstrated so wonderfully for so many centuries? *She can and eventually she will.* Her brilliant intellect (when turned to the study of the things of the spirit) can outstrip the researchings of lesser minds; that clear perception and ability to convey thoughts in concise and crystal clear terms will be utilized to bring home to many the eternal verities. When France finds her spiritual soul and not just her intellectual soul, she will prove to be the medium through which will come revelation as to the nature of the soul of man. France has in the past revealed the nature of the human soul in its stage of intensest individualism and selfishness. Through fire and pain, France will later demonstrate the qualities of the spirit of man. The accent upon the material values and the intense emphasis upon the importance of France to the world, instead of the importance of the international attitude to France in terms of unselfish human relations, summarizes the *psychological problem with which France is at this time faced* and which certain of her finest thinkers realize. Can France learn to think in terms of and for those who lie beyond her boundaries, or will she continue to think in terms of France? These are the questions she must answer.

GERMANY

Of the faults of the German nation, there is little need to speak; they have been made painfully clear to the entire world. The Germany of the mystical poets and writers of the Middle Ages will again arise—the Germany of the musical festivals, the Germany which has given the world the best of the music of all time, the Germany of Schiller and of Goethe and the Germany of the philosophers. The major fault of the German people is an extreme negativity which makes them the most easily "conditioned" people of all time, plus an ability to accept dictatorship and propaganda without any questioning or revolt and with a deep sense of inferiority. The German people are consequently easily exploited, easily convinced by those who can shout and threaten; they are easily regimented.

This negativity must be overcome and attention must be paid to the careful training of the individual to think and act for himself and to set great store by his own ideas, and all in a spirit of goodwill. This should be the keynote of all future education of the German people. Given that and given right idealistic propaganda, the German people can develop right habits of thought as easily as they have been led into evil ways and into separative thinking. The regimentation of the German people must not be stopped for a long time to come but its motivation must be completely altered. *Their main psychological problem is to recognize their relation to all other peoples on equal terms.* The major trouble facing the United Nations will be to find the strong and good leader who can enforce that regimentation in a spirit of understanding and goodwill until such time as it is no longer needed and German men and women can think for themselves, and not in response to the propaganda of a group or a military caste. The responsibility of the Allies is great. Will they take advantage of the responsiveness of the German people to propaganda and see that it is properly and spiritually exploited? Will they see that the educational institutions of that unhappy land are placed in the hands of those with a vision of the future, who have a firm determination to train the rising generation to know themselves as *men and not as supermen?* Can they instill into the consciousness of the children of today and of those who will yet be born, the significance and the importance of right human relations? Can they then continue this educational process for a long enough time? Here lies the test of the true intentions of the United Nations. The spiritual potentialities of the German people must not be forgotten. We must look forward towards that which they can be trained to become. Practically speaking, they can more easily be changed under right methods of teaching and conditioning than any other nation in Europe. Germany still expresses the herd consciousness. This must be transmuted into group consciousness—the consciousness of the free individual who collaborates with other men of goodwill for the benefit of the whole.

GREAT BRITAIN

Great Britain has been a great and imperialistic power. Her acquisitive spirit, her tenacity and the firmness of her political manoeuvers in the past have warranted this charge. She has played "power politics" and has become expert in balancing one nation against another nation in order to preserve the status quo and the integrity of the British Isles. She has wrought with diligence for a stability among the nations which will enable her to function smoothly and attain her ends. She has been accused of an intense commercialism and the phrase "a nation of shop keepers" has been applied to her by other nations. The British are frequently disliked by other peoples; their aloof hauteur, their national pride and their attitude of owning the world alienates many. Great Britain carries the sense of caste into all her international relations just as the class distinction system has controlled her internal relationships for ages. These accusations are all based on truth and the enemies of Great Britain can bring due cause to the judgment seat. The British, as a whole, have been reactionary, over-cautious and conservative, slow to move, and apt to be satisfied with existing conditions, particularly if those conditions are strictly British. All these characteristics have been the cause of extreme irritation to other people, particularly the nation which emerged from Britain, the United States. This is one side of the picture. But the British are not anti-social; they have led the way in welfare reforms, instituting such measures as the old-age pension system long before other nations did so. They are deeply paternalistic in their handling of smaller and less developed nations and have really helped them. Being conservative, it is hard for them to know when to withdraw that paternal help. The motto of the House of Wales is: "I serve". The innate tendency of the British race is to serve the nations and the races which are gathered together under the Union Jack. It must be remembered that since the beginning of the 20th Century, great changes have taken place in the thinking of the English people. Old things have passed away; the caste system with its aloofness, its separativeness and its paternalism is rapidly disappearing as the war and labor emphasize essential equality. Great Britain seeks no more territory; she is now a *commonwealth of entirely independent nations.*

The major psychological problem before the British people is to gain the confidence of the world and lead other nations to recognize the existent justice and the good intentions of their thinking and planning. This she had lost during the past few centuries but is now slowly regaining. Her attitude to world affairs today is internationally based; she is desirous of the good of the whole and is prepared to make sacrifices in the interests of the whole; her intentions are just, and her will is towards cooperation; her citizens are brave and sound in their thinking and are disturbed at what the history of the past has brought to them of dislike. If the emergence from a shy and proud reticence were given free play, Great Britain and the other nations of the world could walk the way of life together with little disagreement.

RUSSIA

Russia remains a great enigma for the rest of the world today. Her potentiality for human service and her ability to impose her will on a large scale upon the entire world outstrips that of any other nation. This in itself breeds distrust. Her territory covers a large part of Europe and the whole of North Asia. She has passed through a great and cruel revolution and a subsequent period of readjustment. She is preparing for world collaboration and is evidencing a wish for this to be accomplished *on her own terms*—the terms of a general control of other lands, beginning with the smaller nations upon her western frontier. She is lifting the peoples of her own land from a condition of ignorance and poverty into one of knowledge and sufficiency. Russia is deeply distrusted by the rest of the world, particularly by its conservative elements, and this for two reasons: first, the cruelty with which the earliest stages of her revolution started—the period which we glibly call "Bolshevism"—and, by a subsequent period of a deliberately chosen and determined isolationism behind her closed frontiers. It was, nevertheless, a creative silence. The war then forced Russia to quit her silence for world collaboration. She was forced into participation in the World War. Russia is the home of a germinating revelation of great spiritual value and group significance—a revelation for all mankind. It is the dimly sensed and somewhat inaccurate realization of this which has led to her insidious propaganda.

Russia has created fermentation in other countries before she herself really knows what is the revelation of which she is custodian. Her activity is therefore premature. The true secret of brotherhood (one hitherto unknown and unrealized) is hers to give the world, but as yet she knows not what it is. This fact, that Russia is the spiritual custodian of a revelation, is sensed by the other nations in the world; and the first reaction has been fear, based on certain initial mistakes and her premature activity upon the physical plane. Nevertheless, all peoples view Russia with expectation; they dimly realize that from her will come some new thing, for Russia is rapidly maturing and integrating and will demonstrate that she has much to give.

The world is witnessing the uprising and the surging forward of a nation which has accomplished in a quarter of a century what other nations have taken many generations to work out. Russia is a giant, getting into his stride—a young giant, aware of great possibility, animated by a deeply religious, though unorthodox spirit, handicapped by a combination of oriental traits and occidental purposes, and distrusted by the world, owing to earlier moves falsely taken. These moves were an attempt to infiltrate into other nations, in order to upset their stability and so weaken them that they could be easily swept into the house of humanity which Russia is attempting to build. Russia is inwardly (but as yet unconciously) motivated by a desire to bring brotherhood into being. Can you accept this diagnosis of that great unknown quantity which is Russia? Time alone can prove the accuracy of this statement, plus wise activity and sound propaganda on the part of Russia. The psychological problem of the U.S.S.R. is, in the last analysis, to mind her own business, to stabilize and integrate a vast population, and to lead her peoples still further into the light. Russia must also learn to cooperate with other powers on an equal basis. Russia must not, with ambition and design, seek to sweep the small powers into her arena of activity against their wishes or through undue pressure and force. Russia has still much to do for the immense territories and their inhabitants which are already within her sphere of influence; the other nations must also work out their own destiny and must not be ruled perforce by Russia. Above everything else, the problem before Russia is to give to the other nations of the world such an example of wise rule, free expression of individual purpose, and the use of an inclusive and sound education, that other nations will pattern themselves upon what Russia has demonstrated, yet will at the same time preserve their own cultural approach, their own self-chosen form of government, and their own mode of expressing brotherhood. Russia inherently stands for a new world consciousness, and through her means, a new planetary expression will gradually be wrought out in the fire of experiment and experience. That great nation (a synthesis of East and West) must learn to rule without cruelty, without infringing the free will of the individual and because she has complete confidence in the beneficence of the ideals which she is developing but which are not yet expressed.

POLAND

As for the Polish people, a long historical past lays upon them the responsibility of a definitely cultural effect upon surrounding nations and of a spiritual giving of which they are as yet apparently unaware. Their continued emphasis upon territorial possessions blinds their eyes to the true value of their possible world contribution. Being a strongly emotional and individual people, they are, within their own borders, in a state of constant disunion and friction; they have no interior unity. Their psychological problem is to achieve an integration which will be based upon the overcoming of racial hatreds. They need to resolve their national problem in terms of goodwill and not of selfish interests. Their real problem is the attaining of right internal relationships.

Although the problem of boundaries, possessions, territories, colonies, and material undertakings loom large in the eyes of all nations, the fact that the emphasis is so purely material indicates its relative unimportance, when seen in true perspective. The only factor that truly matters at this time is *humanity* itself, and in the face of human agony, human distress, and human destitution, the emphasis upon boundaries is stupidly over-emphatic. Adjustments have to be made; boundaries will have to be determined. The ultimate decisions, however, must not be made on the basis of history or of ancient glory, but on the basis of what is best for the peoples involved. They themselves must determine the issue.

The World War has been presented by the finest minds and the idealists among the Allied Nations as being fought ostensibly for human freedom, yet *all* the great Powers entered this war with selfish motives and for self-preservation; this is universally acknowledged. All have a sound and selfless underlying idealism in a greater or lesser degree. This is the freeing of humanity from dictatorship. After war comes the test of the *success of victory*. If the nations throughout the world reap the benefits of free election, if peoples in disputed areas are permitted by a free plebiscite to decide their own loyalties and adherences, and if freedom of speech, freedom of religion and a truly free press and radio are the outcome of this war, a great step forward will have been made by the entire human family.

THE UNITED STATES

The psychological problem with which the United States of America is confronted is that of learning to shoulder worldwide responsibility. Both Great Britain and Russia have already learned that lesson in some form.

The American people—as they pass out of the stage of adolescence—must learn the lessons of life through experimentation and resultant experience. This is a lesson that all young people have to learn. The German race is old; the German nation is very young. The Italian people are of ancient origin; the Italian state is historically of very recent date. The accusation of youth (if it is an accusation) is also true of the United States. A great future lies ahead of that nation but not because of material power or commercial efficiency, as many materially-minded people think. The reason lies in a deeply spiritual, innate idealism, enormous humanitarian potentiality and—above all else—because virgin and non-effete stock of largely peasant and middle class origin is determining the race. Steadily in all nations, the power in government and in determining practical ideologies is rapidly passing into the hands of the "people" and out of the hands of the so-called ruling classes and the aristocracy. Countries such as Great Britain and France, which have accepted the determining evolutionary tendencies, can move forward with greater ease into the future than can such countries as Spain and Poland which have been ruled for centuries by a dominant aristocracy and a politically-minded church. The United States of America has no such handicap, except insofar as the laws of capital and finance seek control. The same is largely true of Great Britain.

' The roots of the people in the United States are necessarily in other countries because its citizens have originally come out of those countries. They have no indigenous people except the Red Indian who has been ruthlessly dispossessed by the on-rushing tide from other lands. The racial groups within the States still bear the marks of their origin and of their racial heritage; they are psychologically and physically of Italian, British, Finnish, German and other origins. In this fact consists part of the wonder of this rapidly integrating nation.

Like all young people, symbolically speaking, the people of the United States show all the characteristics of adolescence. Again, symbolically speaking, the people of the United States are of the ages seventeen to twenty-four. They shout freedom and still are not free; they refuse to be told what to do because it infringes upon their rights, nevertheless they allow themselves to be guided frequently by the inept, the partisan politician and by the inadequate; they are broadly tolerant and yet most intolerant of other nations; they are ready to tell other nations how to handle their problems but as yet evidence no ability to handle their own, as witness the treatment of the American Negroes and the withholding of equal freedom and opportunity from them. They are restlessly experimenting with all phases of life, with every kind of idea and all kinds of relationships. The creative power of the race shows itself as yet in a wonderful control of nature and in great construction projects which bring water under control, or which relate all parts of this vast country through roads and waterways. America is a great battleground for experiment along creative lines; it is profoundly interested in trying out every kind of ideology. The fight between capital and labor will reach its climax in the United States, but will also be fought out in Great Britain and France. Russia already has her own solution but the lesser nations of the world will be guided and conditioned by the result of this battle in the British Commonwealth of Nations and in the United States.

Order must be brought about in the States and this order will come when freedom is interpreted in terms of *self-chosen* discipline; a freedom which can turn into license and which is interpreted by each individual in the best interests of himself constitutes a danger to be avoided. It is a danger of which the best minds are deeply aware.

Like all young people, Americans feel superior to more mature fellow nations; they are apt to think that they have a higher idealism, a saner outlook and a greater love of freedom than other nations; they are apt to forget that though there may be some backward nations, there are many nations in the world with as high an idealism, as sound a body of motives, and with a more mature and experienced approach to world problems. Again, like all young people, the American is intensely critical of other people, but often blind to and always resentful of criticism. Yet there is as much to criticize in America as there is in any other nation; all nations have a vast house cleaning to do, and the difficulty at this time is that they must do it alongside of the strict fulfilling of their international relationships. No nation can live unto itself today. If it attempts to do so it treads the way of death and that is the true horror of the isolationist position. Factually today we have one world and this sums up *the psychological problem of humanity*. The goal is right human relations; nations will stand or fall just in so far as they measure up to that vision. The era ahead of us—under evolutionary law and the will of God—is to see the establishment of right human relations.

We are entering a vast experimental period of discovery; we shall discover just exactly what we are—

as nations, in our group relationships, through our expression of religion and in our mode of governments. It will be an intensely difficult era and will be only successfully lived through if each nation will recognize its own internal defects and will handle them with vision and deliberate humanitarian purpose. This means for each nation the overcoming of pride and the attainment of interior unity. Each country today is divided within itself by warring groups—idealists and realists, political parties and far-sighted statesmanship, religious groups, fanatically occupied with their own ideas, capital and labor, isolationists and internationalists, people violently against certain groups or nations and others working on behalf of them. The only factor which can eventually and in due time bring harmony and the end of these chaotic conditions is right human relations.

Every country also has much to contribute but as long as that contribution is considered, as it now is, in terms of its commercial value or its political usefulness, that contribution will not be given in aid of right human relations.

Every country must also receive from all other countries. This involves a recognition of certain specific lacks, plus a willingness to take from others on terms of equality. Every country has its own peculiar note which must be brought into unison and swell the great chorus from all the nations. This will only be possible when pure religion is restored and the spiritual impetus, nascent in every nation, is given free expression. This is not yet the case; theological forms still hold the spiritual life.

Every nation, owing to its past history, and to its own deeds and enactments, is closely related to every other nation, and of this fact the U.S.A. is perhaps more expressive than many, because its nationals have come from all the known races. Isolationism was defeated even before it reared its ugly head because the people of America are international by origin and background.

Humanity, as has been said before, is the world disciple; the impulse behind the disintegration of the old world forms is a spiritual one. The spiritual life of humanity is now so strong that it has disrupted all present forms of human expression. The world of the past has gone and gone forever, and the new world of forms has not yet made its appearance. Its construction will be distinctive of the emerging creative life of the spirit of man. The important factor to bear in mind is that it is one spirit and the nations have each to learn to recognize that spirit within themselves and within each other.

To sum up: the task of every nation is, therefore, a twofold one—

1. *To solve its own psychological internal problems.* This it does by recognition of their existence; by the quelling of national pride and by taking those steps which would establish unity and beauty of rhythm in the life of its peoples.

2. *To foster the spirit of right relations.* This is accomplished by the recognition of the one world of which it is a part. This later involves also the taking of those steps which would enable it to enrich the whole world with its own individual contribution.

These two activities—national and international— must proceed side by side with the emphasis upon the work of practical Christianity, and not by dominant theologies and subtly imposed Church controls.

From the angle of the spiritual Forces of Light, the immediate world process should include:

1. The impending crisis of freedom. This involves free elections in all countries to determine the type of government, the national boundaries (where that prob-

lem exists) and a plebiscite of the people to determine their nationalities and loyalties.

2. The cleaning up process carried on in all the nations without any exception whatever so that a wholesome unity, based on freedom and demonstrating unity in diversity, can be brought about.

3. A steadily pursued educational process by which all the peoples in the world can be grounded in the only ideology that will prove finally and generally effective—that of right human relations.   Slowly but surely, this educational movement will inevitably produce right understanding and correct attitudes and activities in every community, in every church and nation, and ultimately in the international field. This will take time but it presents a challenge to all men of goodwill throughout the world.

The spiritual guides of the race can present this formula of progress. They cannot guarantee its enactment, for humanity is left free to decide its own problems. Certain questions, therefore, emerge immediately.

Will the great powers, Russia, the United States, and the British Commonwealth of Nations stand *together* for the total good of humanity, or will they each proceed upon their separate way towards their own selfish objectives?

Will the smaller powers as well as the great Powers be willing to relinquish some of their so-called sovereignty in the interests of the whole? Will they attempt to view the world situation from the angle of humanity, or will they only see their own individual good?

Will they omit the constant carping criticism which has distinguished the past and which breeds a growing hatred, and recognize that all nations are made up of human beings, at different stages of evolution, and conditioned by their background, race and environment? Will they be willing to leave each other free to shoulder individual responsibility and yet be willing ever to assist each other as members of one family and as animated by one human spirit, the spirit of God?

Will they be willing to share the produce of the earth, knowing it belongs to all, freely distributing it as nature does? Or will they permit it to fall into the hands of a few powerful nations or a mere handful of powerful men and financial experts?

Such are only a few of the questions for which answers must be sought and found. The task looks hard indeed.

Yet there are enough spiritually minded people in the world today to change world attitudes and to bring in the new spiritually creative period. Will these men and women of vision and goodwill arise in their might in every nation and make their voices heard? Will they have the strength, the persistence and the courage to overcome defeatism, to break the chain of hampering theologies—political, social, economic and religious— and work for the good of all peoples? Will they overcome the forces arrayed against them through firm conviction of the stability and potentiality of the human spirit? Will they have faith in the intrinsic worth of humanity? Will they realize that the entire trend of the evolutionary process is sweeping them on to victory? The firm establishment of right human relations is already a determined part of divine purpose and nothing can arrest its eventual appearance. That appearance can, however, be hastened by right and selfless action.

CHAPTER II

THE PROBLEM OF THE CHILDREN
OF THE WORLD

THIS problem is, without exception, the most urgent confronting humanity today. The future of the race lies in the hands of the young people everywhere. They are the parents of the coming generations and the engineers who must implement the new civilization. What we do with them and for them is momentous in its implications; our responsibility is great and our opportunity unique.

This chapter deals with the children and adolescents, under sixteen years old. These two groups are the most hopeful element in a world which has fallen to pieces before our eyes. They are the guarantee that our world can be rebuilt and—if we have learned anything from past history and its dire consequences in our lifetime—rebuilt along different lines, with different objectives and incentives and with well-defined goals and carefully considered ideals.

Let us remember, however, that visionary, mystical hopes and dreams, wishful thinking and the formulation of highly organized plans upon paper are useful as far as they indicate interest, a sense of responsibility and possible objectives but they are of small importance in any effective, transitional enterprise unless there is a grasp of the immediate problem and of the immediate possibilities, plus a willingness to effect those compromises which will lay the ground for later successful work. This work is largely that of education. Hitherto, there has been little effort to bring about a bridging between the needs of the future and the present forms of education. These forms have apparently failed to equip humanity for successful and cooperative living and the newer aspects of mental training; no scientific bridging has been done and little attempt has been made to correlate the best of the present methods (and not all are bad) with future ways of developing the youth of the world so that it can cope with a new civilization which is inevitably upon its way. The visionary idealist has hitherto held the field against the established modes of teaching; his impracticality and his refusal to compromise has thus slowed up the process and humanity has paid the price. The day has now come when the practical mystic and the man of high mental development as well as of spiritual vision will take his place, thus providing a training which will enable the youth of any nation to integrate successfully into the world picture.

We start with the realization that our educational systems have not been adequate; they have failed to train children for right living; they have not inculcated those methods of thinking and acting which will lead to right human relations—those relations which are so essential to happiness, to success and to a full experience in any chosen sphere of human enterprise.

The best minds and the clearest thinkers in the educational field are constantly endorsing these ideas; the progressive movements in education have done something to remove old abuses and to instill new techniques, but they still constitute so small a minority that they are relatively ineffectual. It is well to bear in mind that had the teaching given to the young during the past few hundred years been of a different nature, the world war might never have happened.

Many and differing reasons have been given for the total war which engulfed us. This has raised the question whether the failure of our educational systems or the ineptitude of the churches may not be the basic causes behind the others. But—the war happened. Our old civilization has been swept away. There are those who would like to see that civilization return and the old structure again rebuilt; they yearn for a peaceful return to the situation before the war. They must not be allowed to rebuild along the old lines or to use the old blueprints, even though necessarily we must build upon the old foundations. It is the task of the educators to prevent this.

Let us be willing to recognize that those countries in which the old mode of education is still peacefully practiced may be not only dangerous to themselves because they are perpetuating the bad old ways, but that they also constitute a menace to those countries which are in the happy position of being able to change their educational institutions and thus inaugurate a better way of preparing their youth for total living. *Education is a deeply spiritual enterprise.* It concerns the whole man and that includes his divine spirit.

Education in the hands of any church would spell disaster. It would feed the sectarian spirit, foster the conservative, reactionary attitudes so strongly endorsed, for instance, by the Catholic Church and the fundamentalists in the Protestant churches. It would train bigots, build barriers between man and man and eventually lead to a powerful and inevitable swing away from all religion on the part of those who would finally learn to think as they reach adult manhood. This is *not* an indictment of religion. It is an indictment of the past methods of the churches and of the old theologies which have failed to present Christ as He essentially is, which have worked for riches, prestige, and political power and which have striven with all available means to increase their membership and to imprison the free spirit in man. There are wise and good churchmen today who realize this and who are steadfastly working for the new age approach to God, but they are relatively few in number. Nevertheless, they are waging war against theological crystallization and academic pronouncements. They will inevitably succeed and thus salvage the religious spirit.

Then let us endeavor to see what the goal of the new educational movement should be and what are the signposts on the way to that goal. Let us try to formulate a long range plan which will meet with no hindrance from the methods immediately employed, which will link the past and the future by using all that is true, beautiful and good (inherited from the past) but which will emphasize certain basic objectives which have hitherto been largely ignored. These newer techniques and methods must be developed gradually and will hasten the process of integrating the whole man.

There is no hope for the future world except in a humanity which accepts the *fact* of divinity, even whilst repudiating theology, which recognizes the presence of the *living* Christ, whilst rejecting man-made interpretations of Him and of His message, and which emphasizes the authority of the human soul.

The future which lies ahead is full of promise. Let us base our optimism upon humanity itself. Let us recognize the self-proven fact that there is a peculiar quality in every man, an innate, inherent characteristic to which one may give the name "mystical perception". This characteristic connotes an undying, though oft unrecognized, sense of divinity; it involves the constant possibility to vision and contact the soul and to grasp (with increasing aptitude) the nature of the universe. It enables the philosopher to appreciate the world of meaning and—through that perception—to touch Reality. It is, above all else, the power to love and to go out towards that which is other than the self. It confers the ability to grasp ideas. The history of mankind is fundamentally the history of the growth of ideas, progressively realized and of man's determination to live by them; with this power goes the capacity to sense the unknown, to believe in the unproveable, to seek, search and demand the revelation of that which is hidden and undiscovered and which—century after century owing to this demanding spirit of investigation—*is* revealed. It is the power to recognize the beautiful, the true and the good and by means of the creative arts to prove their existence. It is this inherent, spiritual faculty which has produced all the great Sons of God, all truly spiritual people, all artists, scientists, humanitarians and philosophers and all who, with sacrifice, love their fellowmen.

Here lie the grounds for optimism and courage on the part of all true educators and here is the true incentive to all their efforts.

The Present Problem of Youth

The world, as known to people over forty years of age, has crumbled and is fast disappearing. The old values are fading out and what we call "civilization" (that civilization we have thought so wonderful) is vanishing. Some of us are thankful it is so. Others regard it as a disaster. All of us are distressed that the means of its dissolution have brought so much agony and suffering to humanity everywhere.

Civilization might be defined as the reaction of humanity to the purpose and the activities of a particular world period and its type of thinking. In each age, some idea functions and expresses itself in both racial and national idealisms. Its basic trend down the centuries has produced our modern world and this has been materialistic. The aim has been physical comfort; science and the arts have been prostituted to the task of giving man a comfortable and if possible a beautiful environment; all the products of nature have been subordinated to giving humanity *things*. The aim of education, generally speaking, has been to equip the child to compete with his fellow citizens in "making a living", in accumulating possessions and in being as comfortable and successful as possible.

This education has also been primarily competitive, nationalistic and, therefore, separative. It has trained the child to regard the material values as of major importance, to believe that his particular nation is also of major importance and that every other nation is secondary; it has fed pride and fostered the belief that he, his group and his nation are infinitely superior to other people and peoples. He is taught consequently to be a one-sided person with his world values wrongly adjusted and his attitudes to life distinguished by bias and prejudice. The rudiments of the arts are taught him in order to enable him to function with the needed efficiency in a competitive setting and in his particular vocational environment. Reading, writing and elementary arithmetic are regarded as minimum requirements, plus some knowledge of historical and geographical events. Some of the literature of the world is also brought to his attention. The general level of civilized information is relatively high, but it is biased and influenced by religious and national prejudices which are instilled into the child from his earliest years, *but which are not innate*. World citizenship is not emphasized; his responsibility to his fellowmen is systematically ignored; his memory is developed through the impartation of uncorrelated facts—most of them unrelated to daily living.

Our present civilization will go down in history as grossly materialistic. There have been many material epochs in history but none so generally widespread as the present or which have involved such untold millions.

We are constantly told that the cause of this war is economic; that is surely so but the reason is that we have demanded so much of comfort and of "things" in order to live "reasonably well". We require so much more than our forefathers needed; we prefer a soft and relatively easy life; the pioneering spirit (which is the background of all nations) has faded, in most cases, into a soft civilization. This is particularly true of the Western hemisphere. Our standard of civilized living is far too high from the standpoint of possessions and far too low from the angle of the spiritual values, or when subjected to an intelligent sense of proportion. *Our modern civilization will not stand up to the acid test of value.* A nation is today regarded as civilized when it sets a value on mental development, when it puts a premium on analysis and criticism and when all its resources are directed towards the satisfying of physical desire, towards the production of material things and towards the implementing of material purposes as well as towards dominating competitively in the world, towards the amassing of riches, the acquiring of property, the achievement of a high standard of material living and towards the cornering of the produce of the earth—largely for the benefit of certain groups of ambitious and wealthy men.

This is a drastic generalization but it is basically correct in its main implications, though incorrect where individuals are concerned. For this sad and dire situation (entirely of humanity's own making) we pay the penalty of war. Neither the churches nor our educational systems have been sound enough in their presentation of truth to offset this materialistic tendency. The tragedy is that the children of the world have paid and are paying the price of our wrongdoing. War has its roots in greed; material ambition has motivated all the nations without exception; all our planning has been directed to the organization of the national life so that material possession, competitive supremacy and individual and national selfish interests would control. All nations, in their own way and degree, have contributed to this; none has clean hands and hence war. *Humanity has the habit of selfishness* and an inherent love of material possessions. This has produced our modern civilization and, for this reason, it is being changed.

The cultural factor in any civilization is its preservation and consideration of all the best the past has given, and its evaluation and study of the arts, the literature, the music and the creative life of all nations—past and present. It concerns the refining influence of these factors upon a nation and upon those individuals in a nation who are so situated (usually financially) that they can profit from them and appreciate them. The knowledge and understanding thus gained enable the man of culture to relate the world of meaning (as inherited from the past) to the world of appearances in which he lives and to regard them as one world, but one existing primarily for his individual benefit. When, however, to an appreciation of our planetary and racial inheritance, both creative and historical, he adds an understanding of the spiritual and moral values, then we have an approximation to what the truly spiritual man is intended to be. In relation to the total population of the planet, such men are few and far between, but they guarantee to the rest of humanity a genuine possibility.

Will cultured people realize their opportunity? Will our civilized citizens embrace the chance to build afresh —not a material civilization this time but a world of beauty and of right human relations, a world in which children can indeed grow into the likeness of the One Father and in which man can return to the simplicity of the spiritual values of beauty, truth and goodness?

Yet, facing the worldwide reconstruction demanded and the well-nigh impossible task of salvaging the children and youth of the world, there are those today who are engaged in raising funds to rebuild stone churches and restore ancient buildings, thus demanding money which is sorely needed to restore broken bodies, to heal psychological wounds and to produce the warmth of love and understanding among those who believe that such qualities do not exist!

The Immediate Need of the Children

The magnitude of the problems to be faced may well leave us bewildered and at a loss how to answer the many questions which immediately arise in our minds. How can we lay the foundation for a long range program of reconstruction, of education and development as it affects the youth of the world and thus guarantee a new and better world? What basic plans must be laid which will be appropriate for so many differing races and nationalities? In the face of understandable hatreds and deep-seated prejudices, how can we make a sound beginning?

The ethical and moral values among the children, particularly among the adolescent boys and girls, have deteriorated and the spiritual values will need awakening. There is direct evidence, however, that this spiritual awakening is already sweeping over Europe and that perhaps from that continent may come that new spiritual tide which will turn the entire world to better things and which will ensure that our materialistic civilization has gone, never to return. A spiritual renaissance is inevitable and is nowhere more needed than in those countries which have escaped the worst aspects of war. For this renaissance we must look and make preparation.

The next urgent problem is surely the psychological rehabilitation of youth. It is a question whether the children of Europe, of China, of Great Britain and Japan will ever completely recover from the effects of war. The early and formative years of their lives have been spent under war conditions and—resilient as children are—there are bound to be certain traces left of what they have seen, heard and suffered. There will be exceptions, particularly in Great Britain and parts of France. Time alone will indicate the extent of the damage done. Much can, however, be offset and even obliterated by the wise action of parents, doctors, nurses and educators. It is sad to report that little has been planned by the psychologists and neurologists along this needed line of salvage; yet their specialized work is sorely needed and is as urgent a demand as that for food and clothing.

It is valuable also to remind ourselves in all our planning and with all our good intentions that the various nations, involved in the world war and whose countries have felt the full brunt of occupation, are laying their own plans. They know what they want; they are determined, as far as possible, to care for their own people, to salvage their own children, to restore their own special cultures and their lands. The task of the Great Powers (with their vast resources) and of the philanthropists and humanitarians throughout the world should be to cooperate with these people. It is not their task to impose upon them what they, from the vantage point of their position, believe to be good for them. These nations want understanding cooperation; they want the implements for agriculture, immediate relief in food and clothing, plus the wherewithal to start again their educational institutions, to organize their schools and to equip them with what is immediately required. They certainly do not want a horde of well-meaning people taking over their educational or medical institutions, or imposing democratic, communistic or any other particular ideology upon them. Naturally, the principles of Nazism and of Fascism must be swept away, but the nations must be free to work out their own destiny. They have each of them their own traditions, cultures and backgrounds. They are being forced to build anew but what they build must be their own; it must be distinctive of them and an expression of their own inner life. It is surely the function of the wealthier and free nations to help them to build so that the new world can come into being. Each nation must tackle the problem of its restoration in its own way.

This need not mean disunity; it should mean a richer and more colorful world. It need not mean separation or the building of barriers or the retiring behind walls of prejudice and racial bias. There are two major linking relationships which should be cultivated and which will bring about a closer understanding in the world of men. These are religion and education. In this chapter we are considering the factor of education which has in the past so greatly failed to promote world unity (as the war has proved) but which can in the future so wisely control.

We are today witnessing the slow but steady formation of international groups, banded together to preserve world security, to protect labor, to deal with world economics and to preserve the integrity and the sovereignty of nations whilst committing each and all to a definite part in the work of securing right human relations throughout the planet. Whether we agree or not with the details or the specific commitments proposed, the formation of international advisory councils, and above all, of the United Nations, are hopeful indications of the moving forward of humanity into a world where right human relations are regarded as essential to the peace of the world, where goodwill is recognized and where provision is made for the implementing of those conditions which will prevent war and aggression.

In the field of education some such united action is also essential. Surely a basic unity of objectives should govern the educational systems of the nations, even though uniformity of method and of techniques may not be possible. Differences of language, of background and of culture will and should always exist; they constitute the beautiful tapestry of human living down the ages. But much that has hitherto militated against right human relations must and should be eliminated.

In the teaching of history, for instance, are we to revert to the old ways wherein each nation glorifies itself at the expense frequently of other nations, in which facts are systematically garbled, in which the pivotal points in history are the various wars down the ages—a history, therefore, of aggression, of the rise of a material and selfish civilization and one which has fed the nationalistic and, therefore, separative spirit, which has fostered racial hatreds and stimulated national prides? The first historical date usually remembered by the average British child is "William, the Conqueror, 1066". The American child remembers the landing of the Pilgrim Fathers and the gradual taking of the country from its rightful inhabitants and perhaps the Boston Tea Party. The heroes of history are all warriors —Alexander the Great, Julius Caesar, Attila the Hun, Richard Coeur de Lion, Napoleon, George Washington and many others. Geography is largely history in another form but presented in a similar manner—a history of discovery, investigation and seizure, followed frequently by wicked and cruel treatment of the inhabitants of the discovered lands. Greed, ambition,

cruelty and pride are the keynotes of our teaching of
history and geography.

The wars, aggressions and thefts which have distinguished every great nation without exception are
facts and cannot be denied.   Surely, however, the
lessons of the evils which they wrought (culminating
in the war 1914-1945) can be pointed out and the
ancient causes of present day prejudices and dislikes
can be shown and their futility emphasized.   Is it not
possible to build our theory of history upon the great
and good ideas which have conditioned the nations and
made them what they are?   To emphasize the creativity
which has distinguished all of them?   Can we not present more effectively the great cultural epochs which—
suddenly appearing in some one nation—enriched the
entire world and gave to humanity its literature, its
art and its vision?

The world war has produced great migrations.
Armies have marched and fought in every part of the
world; persecuted peoples have escaped from one land
to another; welfare workers have gone from country to
country, serving the soldiers, salvaging the sick, feeding
the hungry and studying conditions. The world today
is very small and men are discovering (sometimes for
the first time in their lives) that humanity is one and
that all men, no matter what the color of their skin or
the country in which they live, resemble each other.
We are all intermingled today. The United States is
composed of people from every known country; over
fifty different races or nations compose the U.S.S.R.
The United Kingdom is a Commonwealth of independent nations bound together into one group.   India is
composed of a multiplicity of peoples, religions and
tongues and hence her problem. The world itself is a
great fusing pot, out of which the One Humanity is
emerging.   This necessitates a drastic change in our

methods of presenting history and geography. Science has always been universal. Great art and literature have always belonged to the world. It is upon these facts that the education to be given to the children of the world must be built—upon our similarities, our creative achievements, our spiritual idealisms, and our points of contact. Unless this is done, the wounds of the nations will never be healed and the barriers which have existed for centuries will never be removed.

The educators who face the present world opportunity should see to it that a sound foundation is laid for the coming civilization; they should undertake that it is general and universal in its scope, truthful in its presentation and constructive in its approach. What initial steps the educators of the different countries take will inevitably determine the nature of the coming civilization. They should prepare for a renaissance of all the arts and for a new and free flow of the creative spirit in man. They should lay an emphatic importance upon those great moments in human history wherein man's divinity flamed forth and indicated new ways of thinking, new modes of human planning and thus changed for all time the trend of human affairs. These moments produced the Magna Carta; they gave emphasis, through the French Revolution, to the concepts of liberty, equality and fraternity; they formulated the American Bill of Rights, and on the high seas and in our own time and day they gave us the Atlantic Charter and the Four Freedoms. These are the great concepts which must govern the new age with its nascent civilization and its future culture. If the children of today are taught the significance of these five great declarations and are, at the same time, taught the futility of hate and war, there is hope of a better and happier as well as of a safer world.

Two major ideas should immediately be taught to

the children of every country. They are: *the value of the individual and the fact of the one humanity.* The war boys and girls have learned from appearances that human life has small value; the fascist countries have taught that the individual is of no value except in so far as he implements the designs of some dictator. In other countries, some people and some groups—through hereditary position or financial assets—are regarded as of importance and the rest of the nation as of little importance. In still other countries, the individual regards himself of so much importance and his right to please himself of so much moment that his relation to the whole is entirely lost. Yet the value of the individual and the existence of that whole which we call *Humanity* are most closely related. This needs emphasizing. These two principles, when properly taught and understood, will lead to the intensive culture of the individual and then to his recognition of his responsibility as an integral part of the whole body of humanity.

We have touched upon the physical and psychological rehabilitation of the children and youth of the world. We have suggested that the textbooks be rewritten in terms of right human relations and not from the present nationalistic and separative angles. We have also pointed out certain basic ideas which should be immediately inculcated: the unique value of the individual, the beauty of humanity, the relation of the individual to the whole and his responsibility to fit into the general picture in a constructive manner and voluntarily; we have sought to have the futility of war, of greed and aggression emphasized and that we prepare for a great awakening of the creative faculty in man once security is restored; we have noted the imminence of the coming spiritual renaissance.

One of our immediate educational objectives must be the elimination of the competitive spirit and the substitution of the cooperative consciousness. Here the question at once arises: How can one achieve this and at the same time bring about a high level of individual attainment? Is not competition a major spur to all endeavor? This has hitherto been so, *but it need not be.* The development of an atmosphere which will foster the child's sense of responsibility and set him free from the inhibitions which fear generates, will enable him to attain even higher results. From the standpoint of the educator, this will entail the creation of the correct atmosphere around the child and in this atmosphere certain qualities will flourish and certain characteristics of responsibility and of goodwill will emerge. What is the nature of this atmosphere?

1. *An atmosphere of love* wherein fear is cast out and the child realizes that he has no cause for timidity. It is an atmosphere wherein he will receive courteous treatment and will be expected to be equally courteous to others. This is rare indeed to find in schoolrooms or in homes, for that matter. This atmosphere of love is not an emotional, sentimental form of love but is based upon a realization of the potentialities of the child as an individual, upon freedom from prejudice and racial antagonisms and upon a true compassionate tenderness. This compassionate attitude will be founded upon the recognition of the difficulty of daily living, upon sensitivity to a child's normally affectionate response, and upon the conviction that love always draws forth what is best in anyone.

2. *An atmosphere of patience.* It is in such an atmosphere that the child can learn the first rudiments of responsibility. The children being born in this period and who are now to be found everywhere are of high grade intelligence; without knowing it, they are spiritually alive and the first indication of this aliveness is a sense of responsibility. They know they are their

brother's keeper. The patient inculcation of this quality, the effort to make them shoulder small duties and to share responsibility will call for much patience on the part of the teacher but it is fundamental in determining a child's character for good and his future usefulness in the world.

3. *An atmosphere of understanding.* So few teachers or parents explain to a child the reasons for the activities and the demands that are made upon him. But this explanation will inevitably evoke response, for a child thinks more than is realized and the process will inculcate in him a consideration of motives. Many of the things which an average child does are not wrong in themselves; they are prompted by a thwarted, inquiring spirit, by the impulse to retaliate for some injustice (based on the adult's lack of understanding his motivation), by an inability to employ time correctly and usefully and by an urge to attract attention. These are simply the initial gestures of the emerging individual. Older people are apt to foster in a child an early and unnecessary sense of wrongdoing; they lay emphasis upon petty little things which should be ignored but which are annoying. A correct sense of wrong action, based upon failure to preserve right group relations, is not developed but if a child is handled with understanding, then the truly wrong things, the infringements upon the rights of others, the encroachments of individual desire upon group requirements for personal gain, will emerge in right perspective and at the right time. Educators will need to remember that thousands of children have looked on constantly at evil deeds perpetrated by older people; this will have perverted their outlook, given them wrong standards and undermined right senior authority. A child is apt to become anti-social when he is not understood or when circumstances demand too much of him.

A right atmosphere, the imparting of a few correct principles, and much loving understanding are the prime requirements in the most difficult transitional period with which we are faced. An organized way of living will help much but the children we are considering have known little discipline. The work of sheer survival has been the prime preoccupation of their elders and of the children. It will be hard for them at first to react correctly to an imposed rhythm of living. Discipline will be needed but it must be the discipline of love and one which is carefully and exhaustively explained so that the child understands the reasons lying behind this mysterious new order of carrying on. The fatigue, inertia and lack of interest, incident to war and malnutrition, present definite difficulties at first. Educators and teachers will need to impose upon themselves a discipline of patience, understanding and love which will not be easy, for it will be paralleled by a profound sense of the difficulties to be overcome and the problems to be faced.

Men and women of vision in every country must be found and mobilized and they are there; they must have the equipment they need and the backing of those whom they can trust. Too much must not be demanded at first, for the immediate need is not the impartation of facts but the dissipation of fear, the demonstration that love does exist in the world and the inculcation of a sense of security. Then and only then will it be possible to proceed with those more definite processes which will make the long range plan which some of us have visioned a possibility.

The Long Range Plan

Let us now formulate a more extended plan for the future education of the children of the world. We have noted that in spite of universal educational processes and many centers of learning in every country, we have not yet succeeded in giving our young people the kind of education which will enable them to live wholly and constructively. In terms of the last two or three thousand years, the development of world education has been progressively along three main lines, starting in the East and culminating today in the West. In Asia we have had the intensive training, down the centuries, of certain carefully chosen individuals and a complete neglect of the masses. Asia and Asia alone has produced those outstanding figures who are, even today, the object of universal veneration—LaoTze, Confucius, the Buddha, Shri Krishna and the Christ. They have set Their mark upon millions and still do.

Then in Europe, we have had educational attention concentrated upon a few privileged groups, giving them a carefully planned cultural training but teaching only the necessary rudiments of learning to the masses. This produced periodically such important epochs of cultural expression as the Elizabethan period, the Renaissance, the poets and writers of the Victorian era and the poets and musicians of Germany, as well as the clusters of artists whose memory is perpetuated in the Italian School, the Dutch and the Spanish groups.

Finally, in the newer countries of the world, such as the United States, Australia and Canada, mass education was instituted and was largely copied throughout the entire civilized world. The general level of cultural attainment became much lower; the level of mass information and competency considerably higher. The question now arises: What will be the next evolutionary development in the educational world? What will happen after this complete world breakdown and the recognized failure of the educational systems to avert it?

Let us remember one important thing. What education can do along undesirable lines has been well demonstrated in Germany with its wrecking of idealism, its inculcation of wrong human relations and attitudes and its glorification of all that is most selfish, brutal and aggressive. Germany has proved that educational processes when properly organized and supervised, systematically planned and geared to an ideology, are potent in effect, especially if the child is taken young enough and if he is shielded from all contrary teaching for a long enough time. Since that time Russia has used the same system. Let us remember that this demonstrated potency can work two ways and that what has been wrought out along wrong lines can be equally successful along right ones in a wholesome atmosphere of freedom.

We need also to do two things: We must place the emphasis educationally upon those who are under sixteen years of age, and the younger the better and, secondly, we must begin with what we have, even while recognizing the limitations of the present systems. We must strengthen those aspects which are good and desirable; we must eliminate those which have proved inadequate in fitting men to cope with their environment; we must develop the new attitudes and techniques which will fit a child for complete living and so make him truly human—a creative, constructive member of the human family. The very best of all that is past must be preserved but should only be regarded as the foundation for a better system and a wiser approach to *the goal of world citizenship.*

It might be of value at this point to define what education can be, if it is impulsed by true vision and made responsive to sensed world need and to the demands of the times.

Education is the training, intelligently given, which will enable the youth of the world to contact their environment with intelligence and sanity, and adapt themselves to the existing conditions. This is of prime importance and is one of the signposts in the world today.

Education is a process whereby the child is equipped with the information which will enable him to act as a good citizen and perform the functions of a wise parent. It should take into consideration his inherent tendencies, his racial and national attributes and then endeavor to add to these that knowledge which will lead him to work constructively in his particular world setting and prove himself a useful citizen. The general trend of his education will be more psychological than in the past and the information thus gained will be geared to his peculiar situation. All children have certain assets and should be taught how to use them; these they share with the whole of humanity, irrespective of race or nationality. Educators will, therefore, lay emphasis in the future upon:

1. A developing mental control of the emotional nature.

2. Vision or the capacity to see beyond what is to what might be.

3. Inherited, factual knowledge upon which it will be possible to superimpose the wisdom of the future.

4. Capacity wisely to handle relationships and to recognize and assume responsibility.

5. The power to use the mind in two ways:

   a. As the "commonsense" (using this word in its old connotation), analyzing and synthesizing the information conveyed by the five senses.

   b. As a searchlight, penetrating into the world of ideas and of abstract truth.

Knowledge comes from two directions. It is the result of the intelligent use of the five senses and it is also developed from the attempt to seize upon and understand ideas. Both of these are implemented by curiosity and investigation.

Education should be of three kinds and all three are necessary to bring humanity to a needed point of development.

It is, first of all, a process of acquiring facts—past and present—and of then learning to infer and gather from this mass of information, gradually accumulated, that which can be of practical use in any given situation. This process involves the fundamentals of our present educational systems.

It is, secondly, a process of learning wisdom as an outgrowth of knowledge and of grasping understandingly the meaning which lies behind the outer imparted facts. It is the power to apply knowledge in such a manner that sane living and an understanding point of view, plus an intelligent technique of conduct, are the natural results. This also involves training for specialized activities, based upon innate tendencies, talents or genius.

It is a process whereby unity or a sense of synthesis is cultivated. Young people in the future will be taught to think of themselves in relation to the group, to the family unit and to the nation in which their destiny has put them. They will also be taught to think in terms of world relationship, and of their nation in its relation to other nations. This covers training for citizenship, for parenthood, and for world understanding; it is basically psychological and should convey an understanding of humanity. When this type of training is given, we shall develop men and women who are both civilized and cultured and who will also possess the capacity to move forward (as life unfolds) into that world of meaning which underlies the world of outer phenomena and who will begin to view human happenings in terms of the deeper spiritual and universal values.

Education should be the process whereby youth is taught to reason from cause to effect, to know the reason why certain actions are bound inevitably to produce certain results and why—given a certain emotional and mental equipment, plus an ascertained psychological rating—definite life trends can be determined and certain professions and life careers provide the right setting for development and a useful and profitable field of experience.

Some attempts along this line have been undertaken by certain colleges and schools in an effort to ascertain the psychological aptitudes of a boy or a girl for certain vocations but the whole effort is still amateurish in nature. When made more scientific it opens the door for training in the sciences; it gives significance and meaning to history, biography and learning and thus avoids the bare impartation of facts and the crude process of memory training which has been distinctive of past methods.

The new education will consider a child with due reference to his heredity, his social position, his national conditioning, his environment and his individual mental and emotional equipment and will seek to throw the entire world of effort open to him, pointing out that apparent barriers to progress are only spurs to renewed endeavor. They will thus seek to "lead him out" (the true meaning of the word "education") from any limiting condition and train him to think in terms of constructive world citizenship. Growth and still more growth will be emphasized.

The educator of the future will approach the problem of youth from the angle of the children's *instinctual* reaction, their *intellectual* capacity and their *intuitional* potentiality. In infancy and in the earlier school grades, the development of right instinctual reactions will be watched and cultivated; in the later grades, in what is equivalent to the high schools or the secondary schools, the intellectual unfoldment and control of the mental processes will be emphasized; whilst in the colleges and universities the unfoldment of the intuition, the importance of ideas and ideals and the development of abstract thinking and perception will be fostered; this latter phase will be soundly based upon the previous sound intellectual foundation. These three factors—instinct, intellect and intuition—provide the keynotes for the three scholastic institutions through which every young person will pass and through which, today, many thousands do pass.

In the modern schools (grammar or primary schools, high or secondary schools, colleges or universities) there can be seen an imperfect but symbolic picture of the triple objectives of the coming education: Civilization, Culture and world Citizenship or unity.

The primary schools might be regarded as the custodians of civilization; they should begin to train the child in the nature of the world in which he should play his part, teaching him his place in the group and preparing him for intelligent living and right social relations. Reading, writing and arithmetic, elementary history (with the emphasis upon world history), geography and poetry will be taught and certain basic and important facts of living imparted, plus the inculcation of self-control.

The secondary schools will regard themselves as the custodians of culture; they should emphasize the larger values of history and literature and give some understanding of art. They should begin to train the boy or girl for that future profession or mode of life which it is obvious will *condition* them. Citizenship will then be taught in larger terms and the world of true values be pointed out and idealism consciously and definitely cultivated. The practical application of ideals will be emphasized.

Our colleges and universities should be a higher extension of all that has been already done. They should beautify and complete the structure already erected and should deal more directly with the world of meaning. International problems—economic, social, political and religious—should be considered and the man or woman related still more definitely to the world as a whole. This in no way indicates neglect of individual or national problems or undertakings but it seeks to incorporate them into the whole as integral and effective parts, and thus avoids the separative attitudes which have brought about the downfall of our modern world.

It might prove later (when true religion is again restored) that this training will be fundamentally *spiritual,* using that word to mean understanding, helpfulness, brotherhood, right human relations and a belief in the reality of the world behind the phenomenal scene. The fitting of a man for citizenship in the kingdom of God is *not* a religious activity to be handled exclusively by the churches and through theological teaching, though there is much that they can do to help. It is surely the task of the higher education, giving purpose and significance to all that has been done.

The following sequence suggests itself as we consider the curriculum to be planned for the youth of the immediate generations:

Primary education............Civilization .... ages: 4-12

Secondary education........Culture .... ages: 12-18

Higher education..............World citizenship .... ages: 18-25

In the future, education will make a far wider use of psychology than heretofore. A trend in this direction is already to be seen. The nature—physical, vital, emotional and mental—of the boy or girl will be carefully investigated and his incoherent life purposes directed along right lines; he will be taught to recognize himself as the one who acts, who feels and who thinks. Thus the responsibility of the central "I", or the occupant of the body will be taught. This will alter the entire present attitude of the youth of the world to their surroundings and foster, from their earliest days, the recognition of a part to be played and a responsibility to be assumed. Education will be regarded as a method of preparation for that useful and interesting future.

It, therefore, becomes increasingly apparent that the coming education could be defined in a new and broader sense as the Science of Right Human Relations and of Social Organization. This gives a comparatively new purpose to any curriculum imparted and yet indicates that nothing hitherto included need be excluded, only a better motivation will be obvious and a nationalistic, selfish presentation avoided. If history is, for instance, presented on the basis of the conditioning ideas which have led humanity onward and not on the basis of aggressive wars and international or national thievery, then education will concern itself with the right perception and use of ideas, of their transformation into working ideals and their application as the will-to-good, the will-to-truth and the will-to-beauty. Thus a much needed alteration of humanity's aims from our present competitive and materialistic objectives into those that will more fully express the Golden Rule will come about and right relations between individuals, groups, parties, nations and throughout the entire international world will be established.

Increasingly, education should be concerned with the wholes of life as well as with the details of daily individual living. The child, as an individual, will be developed and equipped, trained and motivated and then taught his responsibilities to the whole and the value of the contribution which he can and must make to the group.

It is perhaps a platitude to say that education should occupy itself necessarily with the development of the reasoning powers of the child and not primarily—as is now usually the case—with the training of the memory and the parrotlike recording of facts and dates and un-correlated and ill-digested items of information. The history of the growth of man's perceptive faculties under differing national and racial conditions is of profound interest. The outstanding figures of history, literature and art and of religion will surely be studied from the angle of their effect and their influence for good or evil upon their period; the quality and purpose of their leadership will be considered. Thus the child will ab-sorb a vast amount of historical information, of creative activity and of idealism and philosophy not only with the maximum of ease but with permanent effect upon his character.

The continuity of effort, the effects upon civilization of ancient tradition, good and evil happenings and the interplay of varying cultural aspects of civilization will be brought to his attention and the dry-as-dust informa-tion, dates and names will fall into the discard. All branches of human knowledge could, in this way, come alive and reach a new level of constructive usefulness. There is already a definite tendency in this direction and it is good and sound. The past of Humanity as the foundation for present happenings, and the present as the determining factor for the future will increasingly be recognized and thus great and needed changes will be brought about in human psychology as a whole.

The creative aptitude of the human being should also, under the new era, receive fuller attention; the child will be spurred on to individual effort suited to

his temperament and capacity. Thus he will be induced
to contribute what he can of beauty to the world and
of right thought to the sumtotal of human thinking; he
will be encouraged to investigate and the world of
science will open up before him. Behind all these applied incentives, the motives of goodwill and right
human relations will be found.

Finally, education should surely present the hypothe-
sis of the soul in man as the interior factor which
produces the good, the true and the beautiful. Creative
expression and humanitarian effort will, therefore, receive a logical basis. This will not be done through
a theological or doctrinal presentation, as is today the
case, but as presenting a problem for investigation and
as an effort to answer the question: What is man?
What is his intrinsic purpose in the scheme of things?
The livingness of the influence and the proclaimed
purpose behind the constant appearance of spiritual,
cultural and artistic world leaders down the ages will
be studied and their lives subjected to research, both
historical and psychological. This will open up before
the youth of the world the entire problem of leadership
and of motive. Education will, therefore, be given in
the form of human interest, human achievement and
human possibility. This will be done in such a manner
that the content of the student's mind will not only be
enriched with historical and literary facts but his imagination will be fired and his ambition and aspiration
evoked along true and right lines; the world of past
human effort will be presented to him in a truer perspective and the future thrown open to him also in an
appeal for his individual effort and personal contribution.

The above in no way implies an indictment of past
methods except in so far that the world today itself
presents an indictment; it does not either constitute an

impractical vision or a mystical hope, based on wishful thinking. It concerns an attitude to life and the future which many thousands of people hold today, and among them many educators in every country. The errors and mistakes of the past techniques are obvious but there is no need to waste time in emphasizing them or in piling up instances.

What is needed is a realization of the immediate opportunity, plus the recognition that the required shift in objectives and change in methods will take much time. We shall have to train our teachers differently and much time will elapse as we grope for the new and better ways, develop the new textbooks and find the men and women who can be impressed with the new vision and who will work for the new civilization. We seek here to emphasize principles with the recognition that many of them are by no means new but that they require new emphasis. Now is the day of opportunity.

A better educational system should therefore be worked out which will present the possibilities of human living in such a manner that barriers will be broken down, prejudices removed and a training given to the developing child which will enable him, when grown up, to live with other men in harmony and goodwill. This *can* be done, if patience and understanding are developed and if educators realize that "where there is no vision, the people perish".

An international system of education, developed in joint conference by broadminded teachers and educational authorities in every country is today a crying need and would provide a major asset in preserving world peace. Steps towards this are already being taken and groups of educators are getting together and discussing the formation of a better system which will guarantee that the children of the different nations (beginning with the millions of children now demanding education today) will be taught truth, without bias or prejudice.

World democracy will take form when men everywhere are regarded in reality as equal; when boys and girls are taught that it does not matter whether a man is an Asiatic, an American, a European, British, a Jew or a Gentile but only that each has an historical background which enables him to contribute something to the good of the whole, that the major requirement is an attitude of goodwill and a constant effort to foster right human relations. World Unity will be a fact when the children of the world are taught that religious differences are largely a matter of birth; that if a man is born in Italy, the probability is that he will be a Roman Catholic; if he is born a Jew, he will follow the Jewish teaching; if born in Asia, he may be a Mohammedan, a Buddhist, or belong to one of the Hindu sects; if born in other countries, he may be a Protestant and so on. He will learn that the religious differences are largely the result of man-made quarrels over human interpretations of truth. Thus gradually, our quarrels and differences will be offset and the idea of the One Humanity will take their place.

Much greater care will have to be given in picking and training the teachers of the future and particularly those who, in the war torn lands, will endeavor to bring educational facilities to the people. Their mental attainments and their knowledge of their particular subject will be of importance, but more important still will be the need for them to be free from prejudice and to see all men as members of a great family. The educator of the future will need to be more of a trained psychologist than he is today. Besides imparting academic knowledge, he will realize that his major task is to evoke out of his class of students a real sense of responsibility; no matter what he has to teach—history, geography, mathematics, languages, science in its various branches or philosophy—he will relate it all to the Science of Right Human Relations and will try to give a truer perspective on social organization than has been done in the past.

When the young people of the future—under the proposed application of principles—are civilized, cultured and responsive to world citizenship, we shall have a world of men awakened, creative, and possessing a true sense of values and a sound and constructive outlook on world affairs. It will take a long time to bring this about, but it is not impossible, as history itself has proved. Some day an analysis will be made of the contribution of the three great continents—Europe, Asia and America—to the general unfoldment of humanity. The progressive revelation of the glory of the human spirit still needs expression in writing—its composite glory and not just those aspects of it which are strictly national. It consists in the fact that every race and all nations have always produced those who have expressed the highest possible point of attainment for their day and generation—men who have united within themselves that basic triplicity: instinct, intellect and intuition. Their numbers were relatively few in the early stages of man's unfoldment but today those numbers are rapidly increasing.

It will be only commonsense, however, to realize that this integration is not possible for every student passing through the hands of our teachers. Students will have to be gauged from the three angles which form the background of this chapter:

1. Those capable of being civilized. This refers to the mass of men.

2. Those capable of being carried forward into the world of culture. This includes a very large number.

3. Those who add to the assets of civilization and culture an ability to function as souls, not only in the two worlds of instinctual and intelligent living but also in the world of spiritual values and to do this with a complete triple integration.

All, however, no matter what their initial capacity, can be trained in the Science of Right Human Relations, and thus respond to the major objective of the coming educational systems. Indications of this can be seen on every hand but as yet the emphasis is *not* laid in training teachers or influencing parents. Much, very much, has been done by enlightened groups everywhere and this they have done whilst studying the requirements for citizenship, whilst undertaking research work into social relations and through the many organizations which are trying to bring to the mass of human beings a sense of responsibility for human happiness and human welfare. This work should be started in infancy so that the consciousness of the child (so easily directed) can from its earliest days assume an unselfish attitude towards its associates.

It is bridging work which has now to be done—bridging between what is today and what can be in the future. If, during the coming years, we develop this technique of bridging the many cleavages found in the human family and in offsetting the racial hatreds and the separative attitudes of nations and people, we shall have succeeded in constructing a world in which war will be impossible and humanity will be realizing itself as one human family and not as a fighting aggregate of many nations and peoples, competitively engaged in getting the best of each other and successfully fostering prejudices and hatred. This has, as we have seen, been the history of the past. Man has been developed from an isolated animal, prompted only by the instincts of self-preservation, eating and mating, through the stages of family life, tribal life and national life to the point where today a still broader ideal is grasped by him— international unity or the smooth functioning of the One Humanity.

This growing idealism is fighting its way into the forefront of the human consciousness in spite of all separative enmities. It is largely responsible for the present chaos and for the banding together of the United Nations. It has produced the conflicting ideologies which are seeking world expression; it has produced the dramatic emergence of national saviors (so-called), world prophets and world workers, idealists, opportunists, dictators and investigators and humanitarians. These conflicting idealisms are a wholesome sign, whether we agree with them or not. They are definite reactions to the human demand—urgent and right—for better conditions, for more light and understanding, for greater cooperation, for security and peace and plenty in the place of terror, fear and starvation.

Conclusion

It is difficult for modern man to conceive of a time when there will be no racial, national or separative religious consciousness present in human thinking. It was equally difficult for prehistoric man to conceive of a time when there would be national thinking. This is a good thing for us to bear in mind. The time when humanity will be able to think in universal terms still lies far ahead but the fact that we can speak of it, desire it and plan for it is surely the guarantee that it is *not* impossible. Humanity has always progressed from stage to stage of enlightenment and from glory to glory. We are today on our way to a far better civilization than the world has ever known and towards conditions which will ensure a much happier humanity and which will see the end of national differences, of class distinctions (whether based on an hereditary or a financial status) and which will ensure a fuller and richer life for everyone.

It will be obvious that very many decades must elapse before such a state of affairs will be actively present—but it will be decades and not centuries, if humanity can learn the lessons of the world war, if the reactionary and the conservative peoples in every nation can be prevented from swinging civilization back on to the bad old lines. But a beginning can immediately be made. Simplicity should be our watchword for it is simplicity which will kill our old materialistic way of living. *Cooperative goodwill* is surely the first idea to be presented to the masses and taught in our schools, thereby guaranteeing the new and better civilization. *Loving understanding,* intelligently applied, should be the hallmark of the cultured and wiser groups, plus effort on their part to relate the world of meaning to the world of outer efforts—for the benefit of the masses. *World Citizenship* as an expression of both goodwill and understanding should be the goal of the enlightened everywhere and the hallmark of the spiritual man. In these three, you have right relations established between education, religion and politics.

The keynote of the new education is essentially right interpretation of life, past and present, and its relation to the future of mankind; the keynote of the new religion must and should be a right approach to God, transcendent in nature and immanent in man, whilst the keynote of the new science of politics and of government will be right human relations and for both of these education must prepare the child.

CHAPTER III

THE PROBLEM OF CAPITAL, LABOR AND EMPLOYMENT

IN a unique sense we stand today at the dawn of an entirely new economic age. This is increasingly obvious to all thinking people. Because of the triumph of science—the release of the energy of the atom—the future of mankind and the type of the incoming civilization is unpredictable. The changes which are imminent are so far-reaching that it is apparent that the old economic values and the familiar standards of living are bound to pass away; no one knows what will take their place.

Conditions will be basically altered; along certain lines, such as the distribution of coal and oil for lighting, heating and transportation, is it not possible that in the future neither of these planetary resources will be required? These are two instances of the fundamental changes which the use of atomic energy may make in future civilized living.

Two major problems will grow out of this discovery —one immediate in nature and the other to be later developed. The first is that those whose large financial interests are bound up in products which the new type of energy will inevitably supersede will fight to the last ditch to prevent these new sources of wealth from benefiting others. Secondly, there will be the steadily growing problem of the release of man power from the gruelling labor and the long hours today required in order to provide a living wage and the necessities of life. One is the problem of capital and the other is the problem of labor; one is the problem of established control of the purely selfish interests which have for so long controlled the life of humanity and the other is the problem of leisure and its constructive use. One problem concerns civilization and its correct functioning in the new age and the other concerns culture and the employment of time along creative lines.

It is not useful here to prophesy the uses to which the most potent energy hitherto released for man's helping can or will be put. Its first constructive use was to end the war. Its future constructive use lies in the hands of science and should be controlled by the men of goodwill to be found in all nations. This energy must be safeguarded from monied interests; it must be turned definitely into the usages of peace and employed to implement a new and happier world. An entirely new field of investigation opens today before science and one which they have long wished to penetrate. In the hands of science, this new potency is far safer than in the hands of capital or of those who would exploit this discovery for the increase of their dividends. In the hands of the great democracies and of the Anglo-Saxon and Scandinavian races, this discovery is safer than in other hands. It cannot however be kept in these hands indefinitely. Other nations and races are discovering this "secret of release" and the future security of humanity is, therefore, dependent upon two things:

1. The steady and planned education of the people of every nation in right human relations and the cultivation of the spirit of goodwill. This will lead to a complete revolution of the present political regimes, which are largely nationalistic in their planning and selfish in their purposes. True democracy, at present only a dream, will be founded on education for goodwill.

2. The education of the children of the future in the fact of human unity and the use of the world's resources for the good of all.

Certain nations, because of their international character and the multiplicity of races which compose them, are normally more inclusive in their thinking and planning than are the others. They are more prone to think in terms of humanity as a whole than are the others. Such nations are the United States, the British Commonwealth of Nations and the united Soviet Socialist Republics. Many nations and races constitute these three Great Powers—the central triangle at the heart of the coming new world. Hence their opportunity to guide mankind at this time and their innate responsibility to act as world leaders. Other races have no such inherent capacity. They are not, for instance, successful colonists and are more nationalistic and exploiting in their approach to "subject races". For the three Great Powers, the fusion of the many elements composing their nationals into a united whole has been a necessary conditioning impluse. The basic intention of the United States is the well-being of all within its national jurisdiction and the "pursuit of happiness" is a familiar citation of this intent; the fundamental principle governing British rule is justice for all; the underlying motive of the U.S.S.R. is right living conditions, opportunity for all and the general levelling of all separative classes into one thriving group of human beings. All these objectives are good and their application to the life of humanity will guarantee a happier and more peaceful world.

In every country without exception there are the good and the bad elements; there are progressive and reactionary groups. There are cruel and ambitious men in Russia who would gladly exploit the world for the gain of Russia and who would seek to impose the will of the proletariat upon all classes and castes throughout the civilized world; there are thinking men in Russia and men of vision who are opposing them. There are reactionary and class conscious people in the British

Empire who fear the growing power of the masses and who hang on desperately to their inherited prestige and standing; they would hold back the British people from progress and would like to see the restoration of the old hierarchical, paternalistic and feudal system; the mass of the people, speaking through the voice of labor, will have none of it. In the United States there is isolation, the persecution of such minorities as the Negro race and an ignorant and arrogant nationalism, voiced by some Senators and Representatives with their racial hatreds, their separative attitudes and their unsound political methods.

Fundamentally, however, these three Great Powers constitute the hope of the world and form the basic spiritual triangle behind the plans and the shaping of the events which will inaugurate the new world. The other powerful nations, little as they may like to realize it, are not in so strong a position; they have not the same idealism or the same vast national resources; their national preoccupation limits their world vision; they are conditioned by narrower ideologies, by a greater struggle for national existence, by their fights for boundaries and material gains, and by a failure to offer full cooperation with humanity as a whole. The smaller nations have not quite the same attitude; they are relatively cleaner in their political regimes and constitute basically the nucleus of that federated world which is inevitably taking shape around the three Great Powers. These federations will be based upon cultural ideals and will be formed to guarantee right human relations; they will not eventually be founded on power politics; they will not be combinations of nations banded together versus other combinations for selfish ends. Boundaries and regional controls and international jealousies will not be controlling factors.

To bring about these happier conditions, one major adjustment must be made and one fundamental change brought about. Otherwise no hope of peace will be found on earth. The relation between capital and labor and between both of these groups and humanity as a whole must be worked out. The problem is one with which we are all familiar; it is one which evokes violent prejudices and partisanships and in the clamor of all that is being said and in the violence of the battle it might serve a useful purpose to approach the subject from a more universal angle and with an eye to the emerging spiritual values.

First of all, it must be recognized that the cause of all world unrest, of the world wars which have wrecked humanity and the widespread misery upon our planet can largely be attributed to a selfish group with materialistic purposes who have for centuries exploited the masses and used the labor of mankind for their selfish ends. From the feudal barons of Europe and Great Britain in the Middle Ages through the powerful business groups of the Victorian era to the handful of capitalists—national and international—who today control the world's resources, the capitalistic system has emerged and has wrecked the world. This group of capitalists has cornered and exploited the world's resources and the staples required for civilized living; they have been able to do this because they have owned and controlled the world's wealth through their interlocking directorates and have retained it in their own hands. They have made possible the vast differences existing between the very rich and the very poor; they love money and the power which money gives; they have stood behind governments and politicians; they have controlled the electorate; they have made possible the narrow nationalistic aims of selfish politics; they have financed the world businesses and controlled oil, coal, power, light and transportation; they control publicly or sub rosa the world's banking accounts.

The responsibility for the widespread misery to be found today in every country in the world lies predominantly at the door of certain major interrelated groups of business men, bankers, executives of international cartels, monopolies, trusts and organizations and directors of huge corporations who work for corporate or personal gain. They are not interested in benefiting the public except in so far that the public demand for better living conditions will enable them— under the Law of Supply and Demand—to provide the goods, the transportation, light and power which will in the long run bring in heavier financial returns. Exploitation of man power, the manipulation of the major planetary resources and the promotion of war for private or business profit are characteristic of their methods.

In every nation, such men and organizations—responsible for the capitalistic system—are to be found. The ramifications of their businesses and their financial grasp upon humanity were, prior to the war, active in every land and though they went underground during the war, they still exist. They form an international group, closely interrelated, working in complete unity of idea and intention and knowing and understanding each other. These men belonged to both the Allied Nations and the Axis Powers; they have worked together before and through the entire period of the war through interlocking directorates, under false names and through deceptive organizations, aided by neutrals of their own way of thinking. Today, in spite of the disaster which they have brought upon the world, they are again organized and renewing their methods; their goals remain unchanged; their international relationships remain unbroken; they constitute the greatest menace mankind faces today; they control politics; they buy prominent men in every nation; they insure silence through threat, cash and fear; they amass wealth and buy a spurious popularity through philanthropic enterprise; their families live soft and easy lives and seldom know the meaning of God-ordained work; they surround themselves with beauty, luxury and possessions and shut their eyes to the poverty, stark unhappiness, lack of warmth and decent clothing, the starvation and the ugliness of the lives of the millions by whom they are surrounded; they contribute to charities and church agencies as a salve to their consciences or to avoid income taxes; they provide work for countless thousands but see to it that these thousands receive so small a wage that real comfort, leisure, culture and travel are impossible.

The above is a terrible indictment. It can, however, be substantiated a thousand times over; it is breeding revolution and a growing spirit of unrest. The masses of the people in every land are aroused and awakening and a new day is dawning. A war is starting between the selfish monied interests and the mass of humanity who demand fair play and a right share of the world's wealth.

There are those, however, within the capitalistic system who are aware of the danger with which the monied interests are faced and whose natural tendency is to think along broader and more humanitarian lines. These men fall into two main groups:

First, those who are real humanitarians, who seek the good of their fellowmen and who have no desire to exploit the masses or to profit by the misery of others. They have risen to place and power through their sheer ability or through inherited business position and they cannot avoid the responsibility of the disposal of the millions in their hands. They are frequently rendered helpless by their fellow executives and their hands are largely tied by the existing rules of the game, by their sense of responsibility to their stockholders and by the realization that, no matter what they do—fight or resign —the situation remains unchanged. It is too big for the individual. They remain, therefore, relatively powerless. They are fair and just, decent and kind, simple in their way of life and with a true sense of values, but there is little of a potent nature that they can do.

Second, those who are clever enough to read the signs of the times; they realize that the capitalistic system cannot continue indefinitely in the face of humanity's rising demands and the steady emerging of the spiritual values. They are beginning therefore to change their methods and to universalize their businesses and to institute cooperative procedures with their employees. Their inherent selfishness prompts the change and the instinct of self-preservation determines their attitudes. In between these two groups are those who belong to neither the one nor the other; they are a fruitful field for the propaganda of the selfish capitalist or the unselfish humanitarian.

It might be well to add here that the selfish thinking and the separative motivation which distinguishes the capitalistic system is also to be found in the small and unimportant business men—in the corner grocery, the plumber and the haberdasher who exploits his employees and deceives his customers. It is the universal spirit of selfishness and the love of power with which we have to contend. The war has, however, acted like a purge. It has opened the eyes of men to the underlying cause of war—economic distress, based on the exploitation of the planet's resources by an international group of selfish and ambitious men. The opportunity to change things is now present.

Let us now look at the opposing group—Labor.

A powerful group, representing the capitalistic system, both national and international, and an equally powerful group of labor unions and their leaders, face each other today. Both groups are national and international in scope. It remains to be seen which of the two will eventually control the planet or if a third group made up of practical idealists may not emerge and take over. The interest of the spiritual workers in the world today is not on the side of the capitalists nor even of labor, as it is now functioning; it is on the side of humanity.

For thousands of years, if history is to believed, the wealthy landowners, the institutional heads of tribes, the feudal lords, the slave owners, merchants or business executives have been in power; they exploited the poor; they searched for the maximum output at the minimum cost. It is no new story. In the Middle Ages, the exploited workmen, the skilled craftsmen and cathedral builders began to form guilds and lodges for mutual protection, for joint discussion and frequently to promote the finest type of craftsmanship. These groups grew in power as the centuries slipped by yet the position of the employed man, woman or child remained deplorable.

With invention of machinery and the inauguration of the machine age during the 18th and 19th centuries, the condition of the laboring elements of the population became acutely bad; living conditions were abominable, unsanitary and dangerous to health, owing to the growth of urban areas around factories. They still are, as witness the housing problem of munitions workers during the past several years and the situation around the coal fields both in the States and Great Britain. The exploitation of children increased. The sweat-shop flourished; modern capitalism came into its own and the sharp distinction between the very poor and the very rich became the outstanding characteristic of the Victorian era. From the angle of the planned evolutionary and spiritual development of the human family, leading to civilized and cultural living and to fair play and equal opportunity for all, the situation could not have been worse. Commercial selfishness and wild discontent flourished. The very rich flaunted their superior status in the faces of the very poor, paralleled with a patronizing paternalism. The spirit of revolution grew among the herded, overworked masses who, by their efforts, contributed to the wealth of the rich classes.

The spiritual principle of *Freedom* became increasingly recognized and its expression demanded. World conditions tended in the same direction. Movements of every kind became possible, symbolizing this growth and the demand for freedom. The machine age was succeeded by the age of transportation, of electricity, of railroads, the automobile, and the airplane. The age of communications paralleled this also, giving us the telegraph, the telephone, the radio and today, television and radar. All these merged into the present age of science which has given us the liberation of atomic energy and the potentialities inherent in the discovery. In spite of the fact that a machine can do the work of many men, which greatly contributed to the wealth of the man with capital, fresh industries and the growth of worldwide means of distribution provided new fields of employment and the demands of the most materialistic period the world has ever seen gave a great impetus to capital and provided jobs for countless millions. Educational facilities also grew and with this came the demand by the laboring classes for better living conditions, higher pay and more leisure. This the employers have constantly fought; they organized themselves against the demands of the awakening mass of men and precipitated a condition which forced labor to take action.

Groups of enlightened men in Europe, Great Britain and the United States began to agitate, to write books which were widely read, to start discussions, and to urge the monied classes to awaken to the situation and to the appalling living conditions under which the laboring class and peasantry lived. The abolitionists fought slavery—whether of Negroes or of whites, of children or of adults. A rapid developing free press began to keep the "lower classes" informed of what was going on; parties were formed to end certain glaring abuses; the French Revolution, the writings of Marx and of others, and the American Civil War all played their part in forcing the issue of the common man. Men in every country determined to fight for freedom and their proper human rights.

Gradually employees and laborers came together for mutual protection and their just rights. The Labor Union movement came into being eventually with its formidable weapons: education for freedom and the strike. Many discovered that in union there is strength and that together they could defy the employer and wrest from the monied interests decent wages, better living conditions and that greater leisure which is the right of every man. The fact of the steadily increasing power of labor and of its international strength is well known and a primary modern interest.

Powerful individuals among the union leaders came to the surface of the movement. Some of the employers, who had the best interests of their workers at heart, stood by them and aided them. They were relatively a small minority but they served to weaken the confidence and power of the majority. The fight of the workers is still going on; gains are steadily being made; shorter hours and better pay are constantly being demanded and when refused the weapon of the strike is used. The use of the strike, so beneficent and helpful in the early days of the rise of labor to power, is now itself becoming a tyranny in the hands of the unscrupulous and self-seeking. Labor leaders are now so powerful that many of them have shifted into the position of dictators and are exploiting the mass of workers whom they earlier served. Labor is also becoming exceedingly rich and untold millions have been accumulated by the great national organizations everywhere. *The Labor Movement is itself now capitalistic.*

Labor and Labor Unions have done noble work. Labor has been elevated into its rightful place in the life of the nations and the essential dignity of man has been emphasized. Humanity is being rapidly fused into one great corporate body under the influence of the Law of Supply and of Demand which is a point to be remembered. The destiny of the race and the power to make national and international decisions, affecting the whole of mankind, is passing into the hands of the masses, of the working classes and of the man in the street. The inauguration of the labor unions was, in fact, a great spiritual movement, leading to the uprising anew of the divine spirit in man and an expression of the spiritual qualities inherent in the race.

Yet all is not well with the labor movement. The question arises whether it is not sorely in need of a drastic housecleaning. With the coming-in of labor governments in certain countries, with the growth of democracy and the demand for freedom, with the uprising of the rule of the proletariat in Russia, and the higher educational standard of the race, it might well appear that new, better and different methods may now be used to implement the Four Freedoms and to insure right human relations. If there is a realization that there should be right human relations among nations, it is obvious that such relations should exist also between capital and labor (composed as both groups are of human beings) and between the quarreling labor organizations. Labor is today a dictatorship, using threat, fear and force to gain its ends. Many of its leaders are powerful and ambitious men, with a deep love of money and a determination to wield power. Bad housing, poor pay and evil conditions still exist everywhere and it is not in every case the fault of the employer.

Power in the future lies in the hands of the masses. These masses are moving forward and by the sheer weight of their numbers, by their planned thinking and the rapidly growing interrelation now established between labor movements all over the world, nothing today can stop their progress. The major asset which labor has over capital is that it is working for countless millions whilst the capitalist works for the good of a few. *The norm of humanity lies at the heart of the labor movement.*

We need to grasp somewhat this picture of a worldwide condition of misery, based on both the capitalistic and the labor movements, to see this entire picture realistically and fairly. In some form or another the interplay between capital and labor, between employer and employee and between the monied interests and the exploited masses has been present. With the steam age, the scientific age, the age of electricity and the age of planetary intercommunication, this evil grew and spread. Capital became more and more potent; Labor became increasingly restless and demanding. The culminating struggle was presented in the world war and its aftermath, a thirty year war in which capital implemented the war and the efforts of labor won it.

Certain questions arise. In the answering of these questions, humanity will solve its problems or, if they remain unsolved, the human race will come to an end.

1. Is the capitalistic system to remain in power? Is it entirely evil? Are not capitalists human beings?

2. Will labor itself, through its unions and its growing power, vested in its leaders, become a tyranny?

3. Can labor and capital form a working agreement or amalgamation? Do we face another type of war between these two groups?

4. In what way can the Law of Supply and Demand be implemented so that there is justice for all and plenty for all?

5. Must some form of totalitarian control be adopted by the various world governments in order to meet the requirements of supply and demand? Must we legislate for material ends and comfort?

6. What standard of living will—in the New Age— seem essential to man? Shall we have a purely materialistic civilization or shall we have a spiritual world trend?

7. What must be done to prevent the monied interests from again mobilizing for the exploitation of the world?

8. What really lies at the very heart of the modern materialistic difficulty?

This last question can be answered in the well known words: "The love of money is the root of all evil". This throws us back on the fundamental weakness of humanity—the quality of *desire*. Of this, money is the result and the symbol.

From the simple process of barter and exchange (as practiced by the primeval savage) to the intricate and formidable financial and economic structure of the modern world, desire is the underlying cause. It demands the satisfaction of sensed need, the desire for goods and possessions, the desire for material comfort, for the acquisition and the accumulation of *things,* the desire for power and the supremacy which money alone can give. This desire controls and dominates human thinking; it is the keynote of our modern civilization; it is also the octopus which is slowly strangling human life, enterprise, and decency; it is the millstone around the neck of mankind.

To own, to possess, and to compete with other men for supremacy has been the keynote of the average human being—man against man, householder against householder, business against business, organization against organization, party against party, nation against nation, labor against capital—so that today it is recognized that the problem of peace and happiness is primarily related to the world's resources and to the ownership of those resources.

The dominating words in our newspapers, over our radios, and in all our discussions are based upon the financial structure of human economy: banking interests, salaries, national debts, reparations, cartels and trusts, finance, taxation—these are the words which control our planning, arouse our jealousies, feed our hatreds or our dislike of other nations, and set us one against the other. *The love of money is the root of all evil.*

There are, however, large numbers of people whose lives are not dominated by the love of money and who can normally think in terms of the higher values. They are the hope of the future but are individually imprisoned in the system which, spiritually, *must* end. Though they do not love money they need it and must have it; the tentacles of the business world surround them; they too must work and earn the wherewithal to live; the work they seek to do to aid humanity cannot be done without the required funds; the churches are materialistic in their mode of work and—after caring for the organizational aspect of their work—there is little left for Christ's work, for simple spiritual living. The task facing the men and women of goodwill in every land today seems too heavy and the problems to be solved seem well-nigh insoluble. Men and women of goodwill are now asking the question: Can the conflict between capital and labor be ended and a new world be thereby reborn? Can living conditions be so potently changed that right human relations can be permanently established?

These relationships *can* be established, and for the following reasons:

1. Humanity has suffered so terribly during the past two hundred years that it *is* possible to bring about the needed changes, provided that the correct steps are taken before the pain and agony are forgotten and their effects have passed out of man's consciousness. These steps must be taken at once whilst patent evidences of the past are still present, and the aftermath of world war is before our eyes.

2. The release of the energy of the atom is definitely the inauguration of the New Age; it will so completely alter our way of life that much of the planning at present being done will be found to be of an interim nature; it will simply help humanity to make a great transition out of the materialistic system now dominating into one in which right human relations will be the basic characteristic. This new and better way of life will be developed for two main reasons:

a. The purely spiritual reasons of human brotherhood, of peaceful cooperative enterprise and the constantly unfolding principle of the Christ consciousness in the hearts of men. This may be deemed a mystical and visionary reason; it is already more controlling in its effects than is believed.

b. The frankly selfish motive of self-preservation. The release of atomic energy has not only put into human hands a potent force which will inevitably bring in a new and better way of life, but also a terrible weapon, capable of wiping the human family off the face of the earth.

3. The steady and selfless work of the men and women of goodwill in every land. This work is non-spectacular but surely founded on right principles and it is one of the main agencies for peace.

On account of this energy discovery capital and labor are each faced with a problem, and both these problems will reach a point of crisis in the next few years.

Money, the accumulation of financial assets and the cornering of the earth's resources for organizational exploitation will soon prove utterly useless and futile, provided that these resources of energy and the mode of their release remain in the hands of the people's chosen representatives and are not the secret possession of certain groups of powerful men or of any one nation. Atomic energy belongs to humanity as a whole. The responsibility for its control *must* lie in the hands of the men of goodwill. They must control its destiny and make it available along constructive lines for the use of men everywhere. *No one nation should own the formula or secret for the release of energy.* Until mankind, however, has moved forward in its understanding of right human relations, an international group of men of goodwill—trusted and chosen by the people—should safeguard these potencies.

If this energy is released into constructive channels and if it remains safely guarded by the right men, the capitalistic system is doomed. The problem of labor will then be the major problem of unemployment—a dreaded word which will be meaningless in the golden age which lies ahead. The masses will then be faced by the problem of leisure. This is a problem which when faced and solved will release the creative energy of man into channels undreamed of today.

The release of atomic energy is the first of many great releases in all the kingdoms of nature; the great release still ahead of humanity will bring into expression mass creative powers, spiritual potencies and psychic unfoldments which will prove and demonstrate the divinity and the immortality of man.

All this will take time. The time factor must govern as never before the activities of the men of goodwill and the work of those whose task it is to educate not only the children and the youth of the world but also to train humanity in the major undertaking of right human relations and in the possibilities immediately ahead. The note to be struck and the word to be emphasized is *humanity*. Only one dominant concept can today save the world from a looming economic fight to the death, can prevent the uprising again of the materialistic systems of the past, can stop the re-emerging of the old ideas and concepts and can bring to an end the subtle control by the financial interests and the violent discontent of the masses. *A belief in human unity must be endorsed.* This unity must be grasped as something worth fighting and dying for; it must constitute the new foundation for all our political, religious and social reorganization and must provide the theme for our educational systems. Human unity, human understanding, human relationships, human fair play and the essential oneness of all men—these are the only concepts upon which to construct the new world, through which to abolish competition and to bring to an end the exploitation of one section of humanity by another and the hitherto unfair possession of the earth's wealth. As long as there are extremes of riches and poverty men are falling short of their high destiny.

The Kingdom of God can appear on earth, and this in the immediate future, but the members of this kingdom recognize neither rich nor poor, neither high nor low, neither labor nor capital but only the children of the one Father, and the fact—natural and yet spiritual

—that all men are brothers. Here lies the solution of the problem with which we are dealing. The spiritual Hierarchy of our planet recognizes neither capital nor labor; it recognizes only men and brothers. The solution is, therefore, education and still more education and the adaptation of the recognized trends of the times to the vision seen by the spiritually minded and by those who love their fellowmen.

CHAPTER IV

THE PROBLEM OF THE RACIAL MINORITIES

THE racial problem is badly obscured by its historical retrospect and presentation, much of which is unsound and untrue; it is obscured also by ancient hatreds and national jealousies. These are inherent in human nature but are fed and fostered by prejudice and those who are animated by ulterior and selfish intentions. New and rapidly arising ambitions are also fomenting the difficulty; these ambitions are right and sound, particularly in the case of the Negro. These ambitions are often exploited and distorted by selfish political interests and trouble-making agencies. Still other factors conditioning the racial problem are the economic distress under which so many labor today, the imperialistic control of certain nations, the lack of educational attainments, or a civilization so ancient that it is showing signs of degeneration. These and many other factors are everywhere present, conditioning human thinking, deluding the many affected by the problem and greatly handicapping the efforts of those who are seeking to bring about right action and develop a more balanced and constructive attitude among these minorities. Minorities, along with the rest of mankind, are subject to the unerring forces of evolution and are struggling towards a higher and better existence, towards more wholesome living conditions, towards more individual and racial freedom and a much higher level of right human relations.

The sensitivity of these minorities, the inflammatory condition of their immediate and expressed ambition and the violence and prejudice of some of those who speak and fight for them prevent the majority from approach-

ing their problem with the calmness, the cool calcula-
tion and the recognition of relation to the whole of
humanity which their problem fundamentally requires.
Racial faults are more widely recognized than racial
virtues; racial qualities find themselves in conflict with
national characteristics or world trends and these still
further increase the difficulty. The efforts of well-meaning citizens (and they are many) and the plans of the
convinced humanitarian to aid these minorities are too
often based solely upon a good heart, Christian principles
and a sense of justice; these fine qualities are, however,
often implemented by a profound ignorance of the true
facts, of the historical values and of the various relationships involved. They are also often impulsed by a
fighting fanaticism which borders on a hatred for the
majority who (as the fighting protagonist sees it) are
responsible for the cruel injustices under which the
racial minority labors. They fail to recognize that the
minority itself is not free from faults but is in a measure
also responsible for some of the difficulties. These racial
faults and difficulties are usually frankly ignored by the
minority itself and its friends.

Racial faults may be entirely the result of the point
reached in evolution, of unfair environing conditions and
of a certain type of temperament, as is the case with the
Negro minority in the United States of America, which
leaves them basically *not* responsible for the difficulty;
or the responsibility of the struggling minority may be
far greater than it is willing to admit, as is the case with
the Jewish minority in the world who are an ancient
and civilized people with a full culture of their own,
plus certain inherent characteristics which may account
for much of their trouble. The difficulty again may be
largely a historical one and based upon certain essential
incompatibilities such as those which can exist between
a conquered and a conquering people, between a mili-

tant group and a negative, pacifist group. These can be found existing today between the Moslem and Hindu populations of India—an ancient problem which the British inherited. To all these contributing factors in the problem of the minorities must be added the separative tendencies which the differing religious systems have fostered and which today they deliberately continue to foster. The narrowness of religious creeds is a potent, contributing cause.

At the very outset of our discussion, it would be wise to remember that the entire problem we are considering can be traced back to the outstanding human weakness, the great sin or heresy of separateness. There is surely no greater sin than this; it is responsible for the entire range of human evil. It sets an individual against his brother; it makes him consider his selfish, personal interests as of paramount importance; it leads inevitably to crime and cruelty; it constitutes the greatest hindrance to happiness in the world, for it sets man against man, group against group, class against class and nation against nation. It engenders a destructive sense of superiority and leads to the pernicious doctrine of superior and inferior nations and races; it produces economic selfishness and leads to the economic exploitation of human beings, to trade barriers, to the condition of have and have not, to territorial possessiveness and to the extremes of poverty and riches; it sets an important emphasis upon material acquisitiveness, upon boundaries, and the dangerous doctrine of national sovereignty and its various selfish implications; it breeds distrust between peoples and hatred throughout the entire world and has led since time began to cruel and destructive wars. It has today brought the entire planetary population to its present dire and dreadful condition so that men everywhere are beginning to realize that unless something is fundamentally changed, mankind is practically already destroyed. But who will engineer the needed change and where is the leadership which will bring it about? It is a state of affairs which mankind itself must face as a whole; and by meeting and facing this basic expression of universal wrongdoing, humanity can bring about the needed change and is offered a new opportunity for right action, leading to right human relations.

From the angle of our subject, the problem of the minorities, this sense of separateness (with its many far-reaching effects) falls into two major categories; these are so closely related that it is well-nigh impossible to consider them apart.

First, there is *the spirit of nationalism* with its sense of sovereignty and its selfish desires and aspirations. This, in its worst aspect, sets one nation against another, fosters a sense of national superiority and leads the citizens of a nation to regard themselves and their institutions as superior to those of another nation; it cultivates pride of race, of history, of possessions and of cultural progress and breeds an arrogance, a boastfulness and a contempt of other civilizations and cultures which is evil and degenerating; it engenders also a willingness to sacrifice other people's interests to one's own and a basic failure to admit that "God hath made all men equal". This type of nationalism is universal and everywhere to be found and no nation is free from it; it indicates a blindness, a cruelty and a lack of proportion for which mankind is already paying a terrible price and which will bring humanity down in ruins if persisted in.

There is, needless to say, an ideal nationalism which is the reverse of all this; it exists as yet only in the minds of an enlightened few in every nation, but it is not yet an effective and constructive aspect of any nation anywhere; it remains still a dream, a hope and, let us believe, a fixed intention. This type of nationalism rightly fosters its individual civilization but as a national contribution to the general good of the comity of nations and not as a means of self-glorification; it defends its constitution, its lands and its people through the rectitude of its living expression, the beauty of its mode of life and the selflessness of its attitudes; it does not infringe, for any reason, the rights of other people or nations. It aims to improve and perfect its own mode of life so that all in the world may benefit. It is a living, vital, spiritual organism and not a selfish, material organization.

Secondly, there is the problem of *the racial minorities*. They present a problem because of their relation to the nations within which or among which they find themselves. It is largely the problem of the relation of the weaker to the stronger, of the few to the many, of the undeveloped to the developed, or of one religious faith to another more powerful and controlling; it is closely tied up with the problem of nationalism, of color, of historical process and of future purpose. It is a major and most critical problem in every part of the world today.

As we consider this crucial problem (upon which so much of the future peace of the world depends), we must make an effort to keep our own mental and national attitude well in the background and to see the emerging problem in the light of the Biblical statement that there is "one God and Father of all who is above all and through all and in us all". Let us regard that statement as a scientific one and not as a pious, religious hope. God has made us all of one blood and that God —under some name or aspect, whether transcendent or immanent, whether regarded as energy or intelligence, whether called God, Brahma, the Abstract or the Absolute—is universally recognized. Again, under the great

Law of Evolution and the process of creation, men are subject to the same reactions to their environment, to the same pain, to the same joys, to the same anxieties, to the same appetites and the same urges towards betterment, to the same mystical aspiration, to the same sinful tendencies and desires, to the same selfishness, and to the same amazing aptitude for heroic divine expression, to the same love and beauty, to the same innate pride, to the same sense of divinity and to the same fundamental efforts. Under the great evolutionary process, men and races differ in mental development, in physical stamina, in creative possibilities, in understanding, in human perceptiveness and in their position upon the ladder of civilization; this, however, is temporary, for the same potentialities exist in all of us without exception, and will eventually display themselves. These distinctions, which have in the past set peoples and races so far apart, are rapidly dying out with the spread of education, with the uniting discoveries of science bringing us all so close together and with the power to think, to read and to plan.

All evolution is cyclic in nature; nations and races pass through the same cycles of childhood, growth, manhood, maturity, decline and disappearance, as does every human being. But behind these cycles, the triumphant spirit of man moves on from height to height, from attainment to attainment and towards an ultimate goal which as yet no man visions but which is summed up for us in the possibility of being in the world as Christ was; this is the hope held out to us in the New Testament and by all the Sons of God down the ages and in every land and by all religious faiths.

In considering our theme we need now to do two things: first of all consider what makes a people, a race or a nation a minority, and then consider along what lines a solution may lie. The world today is full of clamoring minorities who—rightly or wrongly—are making claims upon the majority. Some of the majorities are sincerely concerned in seeing justice done to the struggling and appealing minorities; others are using them as "talking points" for their own ends or are championing the cause of the small and weak nations, not from any humanitarian reasons but for power politics.

The Minorities

There are both national and international minorities. In the international situation there are powerful majorities—the Big Three, the Big Four or the Big Five and numerous smaller nations, demanding equal rights, equal votes and equal position. These smaller nations are afraid of the more powerful nations and of their ability to enforce their will. They are afraid of exploitation by some powerful nation or amalgamation of nations, distrustful of favors and support because of future claimed indebtedness, and unable to enforce their will or express their desires because of military weakness and political impotence. You have, therefore, in the world today great and influential nations such as the U.S.S.R., the British Commonwealth of Nations and the United States of America; you have also powers which have been great and then forfeited all right to recognition; you have other powers, such as France and Spain, who are secondary in influence, but resent it greatly, and finally many small nations each with its own individual life, civilization and culture. All of these without exception are characterized by a spirit of nationalism, by a determination to hold on to what is or has been their own at any cost, and all possessing an historical past and local tradition which condition their thinking; all have their own developed or developing culture and all are bound together by what we call modern civilization. It is a civilization at present founded on materialism and one

which has signally failed to instill into men a true sense
of values—the values which alone can bind humanity
together and bring to an end the great heresy of separateness.

All these nations, great and small, have suffered
cruelly during the years of war (1914-1945) and are
doomed still to suffer through the years of immediate
adjustment. Some have suffered more than others and
have the opportunity to demonstrate a resultant purifica-
tion, if they so choose. Others chose an easy way during
the war and abstained from taking sides, losing thereby
a great spiritual opportunity, based upon the principle
of sharing; they will need to learn the lessons of pain
in other ways and more slowly; nations in the western
hemisphere have not suffered in any acute manner, for
their territories have been spared, and their civilian
populations have lived in comfort, ease and plenty; they
too have lost something and will also need to learn in
other ways humanity's great lesson of identification and
non-separateness.

Great and small today face a new world; great and
small have lost faith in the old ways, and few really
wish to see the old manner of life restored; all the
nations, great and small, are fighting diplomatically,
politically and economically for all they can get for
themselves; distrust and criticism are widespread; there
is no true sense of security, especially among the minorities. Some of the great nations, with a sound realization
that there is no peace for the world unless there is
justice for all, are struggling to create an organization
which will give place and opportunity to all nations but
their efforts are largely based on a selfish commonsense; they are founded also upon the knowledge that
material security and a sufficiency of material supplies
must be the result of a compromise between that which
has been and the—as yet—impossible vision of the

idealist. Their objectives, however, are still material, physical and tangible and are presented idealistically but with selfish motives. This is, however, a great step forward. The ideal is universally recognized even if it remains as yet a dream.

As we face the world picture today, we must see it in its true colors and must realize that if the best possible steps, spiritual and material, were to be taken for the smallest and least important of the minorities, it would create a situation which would completely reverse world politics and usher in an entirely new and more enlightened cultural and civilized age. This, however, is not likely to happen; so close are the interlocking selfish interests that the use of a system of perfect justice and fairness in any one case would upset major material interests, infringe the so-called rights of powerful nations, encroach on settled boundaries and outrage powerful groups even in most distant lands.

Today—on an international scale—the battle of the minorities is going on; Russia is reaching out after influence in many directions; the United States of America is seeking to hold the place of paramount control in South America and in the Far East commercially and politically and is earning a name in those countries (rightly or wrongly) as imperialistic; Great Britain is endeavoring to protect her "lifeline" to the East by political moves in the Near East; France is attempting to regain her lost power by obstructing the work of the U.N. and by championing the cause of the smaller nations in Europe. As the Great Powers play politics and angle for place and position, the masses of the people in every land—great and small—are full of fear and questioning; they are worn by the war, sick of insecurity, underfed and frightened as they look toward the future, tired to their very souls of fighting and quarreling, weary of the tyranny of striking workmen, and wanting only to live in safety, to own the necessities of existence, to raise their children in a certain measure of civilized culture and to live in a land where there are sound economics, a living religion and an adequate educational system.

In every country the great sin of separateness is again rearing its ugly head; minorities abound and are abused; cleavages are everywhere to be found; parties are clamoring for attention and adherents; religious groups are spreading dissension and seeking to gain in membership at the expense of other groups; the rich are organizing so as to control the finances of the world; the poor are fighting for their rights and better living conditions; the tyranny of selfish politics permeates both capital and labor.

This is a true and tragic picture. It is, happily, not the only one. There is another; a study of this other picture will lead to renewed optimism and to constant faith in divine planning and the beauty of the human being. In every nation there are those who see a better vision of a better world, who are thinking and talking and planning *in terms of humanity,* and who realize that those who form the various groups—political, religious, educational and labor—are men and women and essentially, if unconsciously, brothers. They see the world whole and are working towards an inevitable unification; they recognize the problems of the nations, great and small, and the difficult situation in which the minorities today find themselves; they know that the use of force produces results which are not truly effective (for the cost is far too great) and are usually transient. They realize that the only true hope is an enlightened public opinion and that this must be the result of sound educational methods and just and exact propaganda.

It will be obvious that it will not be possible to take up the tale of all the minorities in the international field

and deal for instance with the struggle of the little
nations for recognition and for what they consider
(rightly or wrongly) their just rights. The story of the
little nations would take years to write and years to
read. It would be the story of humanity. All we can do
is to recognize that they have a case to be presented and
a problem to be solved, but that justice and fair play,
full opportunity and equal sharing of the world's economic resources will only be possible when certain broad
and general principles have been enforced by the weight
of public opinion.

The problems of two minorities are attracting at this
time much public attention. If they can be solved a
tremendous step forward will have been made towards
world understanding. They are:

1. *The Jewish Problem.* The Jews constitute an
international minority of great aggressiveness, exceedingly vocal, and they also constitute a minority in
practically every nation in the world. Their problem is,
therefore, unique.

2. *The Negro Problem.* This is another unique
problem, with the Negro constituting a majority in that
great (and as yet undeveloped) continent of Africa, and
at the same time constituting a minority in the United
States of America and one which is attracting great attention. This problem is unique in the sense that it is essentially the problem of the white people and one which
they must solve because they produced it and have perpetuated it.

If we can get some idea of the significance of these
problems, materially and spiritually, and can gain some
insight into the responsibilities involved, much of usefulness may be gained. In the case of the Jews, the
sin of separateness is deeply inherent in the race itself,
as well as among those among whom they live, but for
the perpetuation of the separation the Jews are largely

responsible; in the case of the Negro, the separative instinct derives from the white people; the Negro is struggling to end it and, therefore, the spiritual forces of the world are on the side of the Negro.

1. *The Jewish Problem*

This problem is so old and so well known that it is difficult to say anything about it which will not be in the nature of a platitude, that will not indicate a bias of some kind (from the point of view of the reader) and that will not arouse in the Jewish reader above all an undesirable reaction. There is little usefulness, however, in saying that which will be acceptable or which agrees with all points of view or is a statement of all that has hitherto been said. There are things to be said which are not so familiar and which have seldom been said, or have been said in a spirit of criticism or of anti-Semitism instead of in a spirit of love, as is attempted here.

Let us look for a moment at the situation of the Jews, prior to the bitter and unpardonable attack made upon them by Hitler and prior to the war 1939-1945. They were to be found in every land and claimed citizenship in every country; within the nation of their birth, they preserved intact their own racial identity, their own peculiar way of life, their own national religion (which is everybody's privilege) and a close adherence to those of their own race. Other groups have done this but to a much lesser degree and have been eventually absorbed and assimilated by the land of their citizenship. The Jews have always constituted a nation within a nation, though this has been less marked in Great Britain, Holland, France and Italy than elsewhere, and therefore, in none of these countries has there been any strong anti-Semitic feeling.

In every country and down the ages, the Jew has turned to commerce and has worked with money; they are a strictly commercial and urban people and have shown little interest in agriculture, except lately under the Zionist Movement in Palestine. To their extremely materialistic tendencies they have added a great sense of the beautiful and an artistic conception which has added much to the world of art; they have ever been the patrons of the beautiful, and have also been amongst the world's great philanthropists and this in spite of undesirable and devious business methods, which have made them greatly disliked and mistrusted in the world of business. They are and remain an essentially oriental people—which the occidental is apt to forget; if he remembered it he would realize that the Eastern approach to truth and honesty and to the use and possession of money is widely different to that of the Western, and herein is to be found a part of the difficulty. It is not so much a question of right and wrong as one of different standards and inherent racial attitudes which are shared with the whole of the East.

The modern Jew is also the product of many centuries of persecution and of migrations; he has wandered from country to country and from city to city, and in the course of these wanderings he has inevitably developed certain habits of living and thinking which, again, the occidental fails to recognize and for which he makes no allowance; the Jews are, for instance, the product of centuries of tent-dwelling and hence the untidy effect they have on any community in which they live and which the more organized Westerner (a cave-dweller) fails to recognize. They are also the product of their need, down the centuries, to *live off* the people among whom they wander, to seize the presented chance to take what they want, to see to it that their children get the best of everything available, no matter what the cost to others, to cling to their own people in the midst of the alien races among whom they cast their lot, and to preserve inviolate, as far as may be, their national religion, their national taboos and the ancient landmarks. This has been essential to their existence under persecution; it has been compulsory for them to preserve these factors in their ancient forms as far as possible, so as to provide evidence to other Hebrews in new lands and cities that they were Jews as they claimed to be. It is this that makes them the most reactionary and conservative race in the world.

Racial characteristics have become increasingly pronounced owing to the inevitable intermarriage during the past centuries and the emphasis laid by the orthodox Jew in the past upon racial purity. The young and modern Jew lays no emphasis upon this and has usually no objection to intermarriage with the Gentiles, but this is only a late development which meets with no approval from the older generation. The Gentile also objects in many cases.

The Jew is a good citizen, law-abiding, kindly and decent in his ways, anxious to play his part in community life and ready with his money when asked for it but—he still remains apart. The Ghetto tendency, as one might call it, can be seen spreading everywhere, particularly in the larger cities in the different countries. Down the ages, the Jews for measures of protection and for communal happiness tended to herd together and to seek each other out, and the Gentiles among whom they found themselves fostered this tendency; thus habits of association were formed which still control. Added to this, and due to the separative action of the Gentile world, restricted areas and cities began to appear in many countries in which no Jew was permitted to reside or to purchase property or to settle. Because of the aptitude of the Jew to live off other people and to live within a nation, benefiting by its customs, culture and civilization but retaining a separate identity and not becoming a true part of the national life, the Jew has ever been subjected to persecution; *as a race,* he is nowhere liked and people are on guard against him and his methods.

This general statement is often untrue where the individual Jew is concerned. There are Jews in every nation and locality who are deeply loved by all who know them, whether Jew or Gentile, who are respected by all around them, who are sought after and valued. These belong to the great spiritual aristocracy of humanity, and though they function in Jewish bodies and bear Jewish names, they join forces with men and women gathered out of all nations who belong to humanity and who have outgrown national and racial characteristics. These men and women are, as a group, the hope of humanity, the guarantee of the new and better world for which we all wait; their numbers are increasing daily. In a broad generalization about any race or nation, the individual necessarily suffers, but the statements made about the race or nation *as a whole* are correct, true and verifiable.

Perhaps the major factor which has made the Jew separative and which has cultivated in him the superiority complex which distinguishes him (under an outer inferiority) is his religious faith. This faith is one of the oldest in the world; it is older than Buddhism by centuries; older than many of the Hindu faiths, and much more ancient than Christianity, and there are features in it which have definitely made the Jew what he is. It is a religion of taboos, built up carefully to protect the wandering Jew as he drifted from one community to another; it is a religion with a distinctly material basis, emphasizing the "land flowing with milk and honey"; this was not symbolic in the days of its use, but a presented objective of his travels. The coloring of the religion is separative; God is the God of the Jews;

the Jews are God's chosen people; they must be pre-served in physical purity and their well-being is of major importance to Jehovah; they have a messianic destiny, and Jehovah is jealous of their contacts and interest in any other people or God. To these divine requirements they have, as a people, been obedient and hence their plight in a modern world.

The word "love" as it concerns relation to other people is lacking in their religious presentation, though love of Jehovah is taught with due threats; the concept of a future life, dependent upon conduct and behavior to others and on right action in the world of men, is almost entirely lacking in *The Old Testament* and teaching on immortality is nowhere emphasized; salvation is apparently dependent upon the keeping of numerous physical laws and rules related to physical cleanliness; they go so far as to establish retail shops where these rules are kept—in a modern world where scientific methods are applied to purity in food. All these and other factors of less importance set the Jew apart, and these he enforces no matter how obsolete they are or inconvenient to others.

These factors demonstrate the complexity of the problem from the Jewish angle and its irritating and frictional nature to the Gentile. This irritating factor is something which the Jew seldom if ever recognizes. The Gentile today neither remembers nor cares that the Jews were instrumental in having Christ put to death (according to *The New Testament*); he is more apt to remember that Christ was a Jew and to wonder why the Jew was not the first to claim and love Him. He remembers far more acutely Jewish business methods, the fact that the Jew, if orthodox, regards Gentile food as impure for him and that the Jew considers his citizenship as secondary to his racial obligations. He regards the Jew as a follower of an obsolete religion; he intensely dislikes the cruel and jealous Jehovah of the Jews and looks upon *The Old Testament* as the history of a cruel and aggressive people—apart from the Psalms of David, which all men love.

These are points to which the Jew at no time seems to pay attention and yet it is these things in their aggregate which have set the Jew apart from the world in which he wants to live and be happy and in which he is the victim of an inheritance which could with profit be modernized. Nowhere is the emergence of a new world religion more greatly needed than in the case of the Jew in the modern world.

Yet—God has made all men equal; the Jew is a man and a brother, and every right that the Gentile owns is his also, inalienably and intrinsically his. This the Gentile has forgotten and great is his responsibility for wrong doing and cruel action. The Jew for ages has not been wanted by his Gentile brother; he has been chased from place to place; constantly and ceaselessly the Jew has been forced to move on or move out—across the desert from Egypt to the Holy Land, from there (centuries later) to the Mesopotamia Valley and from that time on in a constant series of migrations, with great streams of wandering Jews moving ceaselessly north, south and west and a small trickle going east; expelled from cities and countries during the Middle Ages, then after a period of relative quiescence again the displaced Jews were on the move in Europe, homeless, drifting hither and thither (along with many thousands of other nationalities, however), helpless in the hands of a cruel fate, or not so helpless but organized by certain political groups for international and selfish ends. In the countries where anti-Semitic feeling has been practically nonexistent for decades, antagonism is rising; in Great Britain its evil head can now be seen, and in the United States of America it is a mounting menace.

It is for the Gentiles to bring the cycle of persecutions to an end once and for all; it is for the Jew to take those steps which will not arouse the dislike of the Gentiles among whom he lives.

The need of the Jew at this time is for a solution of this ancient problem which has disturbed the peace of countries down the centuries. The responsibility of the non-Jews, in the light of humanitarian demand, is vital; the record of the persecution of the Jews is a grievous and ghastly story, only paralleled by the Jewish treatment of their enemies, as related in *The Old Testament*. The fate of the Jews in the world war is a terrible tale of cruelty, torture and wholesale murder and *the treatment of the Jews down the ages is one of the blackest chapters in human history*. For it there is no excuse or condonation, and right thinking people everywhere are aware of this and are eagerly demanding that these persecutions end. The spiritual forces of the world and the spiritual leaders of humanity (both those working on the outer plane and those guiding from the inner side of the veil) are seeking a solution.

The solution, however, will be found only when the Jews themselves seek to find the way out and cease their present policy of demanding that the Gentiles and Christians make all the concessions, find the solution of the problem alone, and, unaided by the Jews, bring the evil situation to an end. The Jews voice loudly and constantly their demand for redress and help; they blame the non-Jewish nations for their miseries; they fail always to recognize any conditions on their own side which could account for some of the general dislike with which they are confronted; they make no concessions to the civilizations and cultures in which they find themselves but insist on remaining apart; they blame others for their isolation, but the fact remains that they have been given equal opportunity as citizens in all open-minded countries. Their contribution to the solution of this ancient problem is a material one, and shows no psychological insight or any recognition of the spiritual values involved; no problem can today be solved entirely along material lines. Man has as a whole outgrown that.

The problem of the Jews goes deeply into the entire question of right human relations; it can only be solved on that inclusive basis. It concerns the interplay between people of different races but recognizing brotherhood in the human family; it evokes the whole problem of selfishness and unselfishness, of consideration and of justice, and these are factors which must condition all parties. The Jew needs to recognize his share in bringing about the dislike which hounds him everywhere; the Gentile must shoulder his responsibility for endless persecutions and pay the price of restitution. The Jew has evoked and still evokes dislike, and for this there is absolutely no need.

To sum up, the Jew has set up an ancient pattern of living within other nations; as a citizen with all the rights of citizenship, he has built up a wall of taboos, of habits and of religious observances which separate him off from his environment and make him non-assimilable. These must go, and he must become a citizen not only in name but in fact. There is no other problem like it in the world today—an entire people of distinctive race, religion, goals, characteristics, culture and a uniquely ancient and most reactionary civilization, scattered as a minority in every nation, positing an international problem, possessed of great wealth and influence, claiming citizenship in every nation but retaining deliberately their racial identity, creating dissension among the nations, attempting in no way to meet harmoniously their complex problem on any large scale with due psychological understanding or consideration of the Gentile en-

vironment to which they ceaselessly make appeal, prof-
fering only material solutions and constant, almost
abusive, demands for the Gentile to shoulder the entire
blame and end the difficulty.

Alongside of this, one must place the long and sorry
story of the persecution of the Jews by the Gentiles—
widespread in the Middle Ages (if one goes no further
back), sporadic in more modern times, but culminating
in the violent treatment of the Jews during the world
war. It was, however, a treatment not uniquely theirs
but meted out also to Poles, Greeks and the helpless of
many nations. This is a point which the Jews today
appear to forget. They have not been alone in their
persecution. The Jews constituted only twenty per cent
of the dispersed persons in Europe after the war.

This same sorry story of Gentile cruelty includes also
the growing anti-Semitism which can be seen even in
countries which have been relatively free from it; there
is a constant discrimination against the Jew in business
circles; restricted areas are increasing everywhere; the
plight of Jewish school children in the U.S.A., for instance, who are discriminated against, hooted at and
abused, is shocking to contemplate. The situation also
exists wherein no country anywhere wants to open its
doors and offer the unwanted Jews asylum. No nation
wants to admit them in their hundreds. Right thinking
people in every nation are seeking and will continue
to seek a solution, and one will be found. This problem
child within the family of nations is a child of the one
Father and spiritually identified with all men everywhere.
People know that there is "neither Jew nor Gentile", as
St. Paul expressed it (facing two thousand years ago
the same sad problem), and men and women in both
groups have constantly and increasingly proved the
truth of this statement.

Such is the problem of the Jewish minority, given with a frankness which will evoke much criticism, but given in this way in the hope that because it is prompted by love, the Jews will shoulder their own responsibilities, will cease crying aloud to the Gentiles to solve the problem *alone,* and will begin to cooperate with a full sense of spiritual understanding and so aid the thousands of Gentiles who earnestly want to help. There has never been a time when the Gentile world has been more keen to do what is right by the Jew or more anxious to solve his problem and make restitution for all he has suffered. Changed inner attitudes are needed on both sides, but very largely on the side of the Jews; there is evidence that these new attitudes are germinating, even if the finding of the right solution may take much time. There are Jews who today are saying what is said here.

2. *The Negro Problem*

This problem is totally different to that of the Jews. In the first case you have an exceedingly ancient people who for thousands of years have played their part in the arena of world history and who have developed a culture and identified themselves with a civilization which has enabled them to take their place on equal terms with what we call the "civilized" peoples. In the case of the Negro, we are considering a people who have (during the past two hundred years) begun to rise in the scale of human endeavor and have, in that time, made amazing progress against great odds and much opposition. Two hundred years ago, the Negroes were all to be found in Africa and are still there in the millions; two hundred years ago, they were what the European and American regarded as "raw savages", divided into countless tribes, living in a state of nature, primitive, warlike, totally uneducated from the modern point of view, ruled by chieftains and under the guidance of tribal Gods, controlled by tribal taboos, differing greatly from each other—the Pygmy and the Bechuanaland warrior would appear to have no point of resemblance except their color—constantly fighting among themselves and raiding each other's territory.

For centuries they have been exploited and driven into slavery, first by the Arabs, then later by those who purchased them from the slave-owners and carried them into slavery to the United States or to the West Indies. They have been exploited also by the European nations who seized vast territories in Africa and enriched themselves on the produce of those countries and the labor of their inhabitants—the French in the French Sudan, the Belgians in the Belgian Congo, the Dutch and the British in South Africa and the West Coast of Africa, the Germans in German East Africa and the Italians in Eastern Africa. It is a sorry story of cruelty, theft and exploitation on the part of the white race, though much good also came out of it for the black race. The story of these relationships is still unfinished, and unless it is conducted in the future with righteousness and justice, may terminate in tragedy. There is, however, much improvement in the internal history of these territories, and there is much reason for optimism.

The problem of the Negro falls into two divisions: the problem of the future of the African Negro and the problem of the future of the Negro in the western hemisphere.

Africa is potential and the destiny of its countless millions of inhabitants is still in the embryonic stage; the relationship of its true inhabitants to the alien races who seek to dominate them remains still in the realm of political maneuvering and commercial greed. It should, however, be recognized that in spite of the many attendant evils which follow ever on the trail of the exploiting white man, the impact of the white races on the "black continent" has brought great evolutionary development and benefits—education, medical aid, the ending of the ceaseless tribal wars, sanitation, and a more enlightened religious system in the place of the barbaric cults and crude religious practices. Much evil followed the explorer, the missionary and the trader but much good also followed in their steps, particularly in those of the missionary. The Negro is naturally religious and mystically inclined, and the major tenets of the Christian faith have a definite appeal to his nature; the emotional aspects of the Christian presentation (with the emphasis upon love and goodness and the life hereafter) is understood by the emotionally focussed Negro. Behind the many separative religious cults of that dark land, there emerges a fundamental and pure mysticism, ranging all the way from nature worship and a primitive animism to a deep occult knowledge and an esoteric understanding which may some day make Africa the seat of the purest form of occult teaching and living. This, however, lies several centuries ahead.

In considering the problem of the African Negro, it is the long range vision with which we must deal and the steady rising into power of millions of people who have, as yet, only made the first steps towards modern civilization and culture, but are taking others with an almost frightening rapidity. The undesirable aspects of civilization are present, but the benefits conferred far outweigh these, and the Negro, in spite of his natural and understandable antagonism, should recognize them as a debt he owes to the aggressive and acquisitive white nations. Contact with them has stimulated his intellectual perception; the white man's way of living has lifted the Negroes of Africa out of their primitive state into a more modern one; education and modern ways of thinking and planning are rapidly fitting the Negroes to take their place in a modern world; science, transportation and knowledge—brought to them through the medium of the white races—are tying them closely into the developing scheme of modern history; the new world with its better ways of living is as much for the Negro as for the white man.

But beyond this necessary recognition of indebtedness and the effort to benefit from the presented conditions and to ignore that which is evil and undesirable, the Negro problem, both in Africa and in the western world, is largely (if not entirely) that of the white race and one which it is their responsibility to solve. In Africa the Negro greatly outnumbers the white population; the latter is in so small a minority that they are faced with a most difficult situation, living as they do in the midst of an overpoweringly vast black population. In the West and in America, the situation is reversed and the Negroes constitute a minority, greatly outnumbered by the white people. In Africa the Negro is virile and militant; in America and the West Indies he has been somewhat emasculated and psychologically defeated by years of forced labor and slavery. Slavery exists also in Africa, but it has been of a different kind and has not produced quite the same results as it has in the West.

The problem facing the white races now in Africa is so to train the Negroes that they will be fitted for true self-government. They must be helped to take over their own destiny; they must be given a sense of trained responsibility; they must be taught to realize that Africa can belong to its own people and at the same time be a cooperating partner in world enterprise. This can only happen when the antagonism between the white people and the black races is ended; between the two of them goodwill must be demonstrated. Right human relations must be firmly established between the emerging Negro empire and the rest of the world; the new ideals and the new world trends must be fostered in the receptive Negro consciousness and in this way "darkest Africa" will become a radiant center of light, ready for self-government and expressing true freedom. Increasingly these Negro races will forsake their emotional reaction to circumstances and events, and meet all that transpires with a mental grasp and an intuitive perception which will put them on a par and perhaps ahead of the many who today condition the environment and the circumstances of the Negro.

We might express the possibilities as follows: Will the Negroes of Africa arrive at control of their own continent by violently ejecting the governing white races and by a long cycle of wars between the different Negro groups which people that continent? Or will the matter be settled by an understanding farsighted policy on the part of the white people, plus cooperative planning for the future? Will this be paralleled by an ability on the part of the Negro races to move slowly and wisely, to avoid bloodshed and rancor, to see through the devious ways of selfish political agents (seeking to exploit them) and demonstrate also such an outstanding capacity to handle their own affairs and produce their own leaders that naturally and automatically, without conflict or violence, they will gather the reins of government into their own hands and gradually eliminate white control? Will the white nations who today commercially exploit Africa, holding on to their land tenure, relinquish their so-called rights (based on the fact that possession is nine-tenths of the law) and substitute the New Age methods of right human relations and intelligent cooperation, the sharing of resources, so rich and varied in that wonderful continent, and contribute their trained skill, their proved commercial benefits and their scientific knowledge to all that Africa has to offer of usefulness and productive materials to the world? The

European nations and the British peoples are now following a program leading to the release of Africa into the hands of its own people. At the same time, a sane patience should lead the African peoples to concentrate on educational processes, and agricultural and economic developments. The destiny of this great land will clarify itself and Africa will take its place as a great center of cultural light, shining within a civilized land.

Unless both races, the black and the white, approach the problem of their relationship with sanity, with long range vision, with patience and without hatred or fear, the cultural history of our planet will be retarded for many years. The hitherto unused and unorganized power of the countless millions of Africa is something that the white race should carefully consider. They can place the Negro peoples as rapidly as possible on an equality of opportunity, of constitutional and human rights, and help them to pass through the stage of adolescence in which they are now to be found to that full and useful maturity in which they will handle their own problems and territory. This process is now going forward and Africa will thus take its place (through its many possible national groups) in the great family of nations and bring into the world arena a race with an amazing contribution to make of spiritual assets, cultural values and creative possibilities.

The innate endowment of the Negro is very rich in content. He is creative, artistic and capable of the highest mental development when taught and trained—as capable as is the white man; this has been proved again and again by the artists and the scientists who have come out of the Negro race and by the fact of their aspirations and their ambitions. The time has come when the white man must cease to look upon the Negro as a field laborer, a factory hand, a beast of burden, or one only capable of housework or unskilled labor and accord him the respect and the opportunity which is due him.

The Negro of Africa is emerging fast and when a few more years of education, study and travel have played their part, the problem of Africa will become even more acute than it already is. It need not become dangerous if the white race demonstrates wisdom, understanding, selfless thinking and a willingness to give complete freedom to the Negro races. The future peace of the world depends today upon enlightened, far-seeing statesmanship and an appreciation of the fact that God has made all men free.

The problem of the Negro in the western hemisphere constitutes a very ugly story, seriously implicates the white man and provides an outstanding disgrace. Brought to the United States and to the West Indies more than two centuries ago and forced into slavery, the Negro has never had a fair deal or any true opportunity. Under the constitution of the United States, all men are regarded as free and equal; the Negro, however, is not free or equal, particularly in the southern states. The situation in the West Indies more closely resembles that in the northern states, where conditions are somewhat better but where there is still no equality of opportunity and much racial discrimination. The treatment of the Negro in the southern states is a blot upon the country; there the fight is to keep the Negro consistently *down,* to refuse him equality of education and of opportunity, to keep his standard of living at the lowest possible level and well below that of the white, to refuse him political recognition and, in a democratic country where all men are entitled to vote, he is prevented from sharing in this constitutional privilege. In the northern states these conditions do not exist to the same extent, but the Negro is steadily discriminated against, is refused equal opportunity and has to fight for every privilege. A few corrupt and ignorant senators consistently outrage the good intentions of the mass of American people by perpetuating these evil conditions and fighting by every possible means to prevent their being changed; they play upon the fears of their constituents and block every move made to bring about a better and cleaner situation which would be *in line with the constitution*. These shortsighted politicians attempt to sidetrack the issue and throw dust in the eyes of their constituents by fighting for the freedom of distant small nations in Europe; at the same time they steadily defy their own constitution by refusing freedom and liberty to the Negroes of their own country. For their attitude and conduct there is today no possible excuse. It remains a mystery in the minds of other enlightened nations why the broad-minded people of the United States—vociferous in their demand for their own personal freedom and insistent upon the defense of the constitution—permit this condition to exist and perpetuate in office these men who bring about a constant infringement of the constitutional rights of American citizens.

The cry of the south that the Negro is not educationally fitted to vote is negated by the fact that he can and does vote in the northern states, in many cases as wisely as his white brother, and though his vote can often be purchased by electioneering politicians so also can that of the white voter; the cry that white women must be protected from the animal instincts of the Negroes means nothing, for they need equal protection from the animal instincts of the white man, and this statistics will adequately prove; the cry that paternalism is what the Negro needs and that only the southerner understands how to handle the Negro is disproved by the Negro himself who wants none of it; his repudiation of it demonstrates a sound sense of values and that he knows the distinction between paternalism (which keeps the

Negro backward, uneducated and under obligation to the white) and the freedom which he wants to share with all men in the world.

The Negro is naturally easy, accommodating, kindly and anxious to like people and be liked; if today so many Negroes are arrogant, vindictive, full of hate and anxious to assert themselves it is because they have been made so by the white people. The white people face a grave responsibility and it lies in their hands to change conditions. When they do so, they will find the Negro as responsive to good and fair treatment, equal opportunity and right living conditions as he is responsive sometimes in the wrong way to the evil educational, political and living conditions under which he now labors. This applies to the entire Negro problem in the western hemisphere.

The Negro cannot be discriminated against for all time; he cannot be asked to defend his country and then have his country refuse him the ordinary rights of citizenship. Public opinion is on the side of the Negro and there is a steadily growing determination among the white citizens of the western hemisphere that he be given his constitutional rights, equal commercial and business opportunities, equal educational facilities and equally good living conditions. It is for the people of America to speak with a clear voice and demand that Negroes be given their just rights. Every white American should shoulder his responsibility for this minority and study the Negro problem; he should learn to know the Negro personally as a friend and a brother; he should see to it that he plays his part in changing the present condition.

On the subject of intermarriage, the best and soundest thinkers in both the white and black races at this time deplore mixed marriages. They mean no happiness for either party. When considering this subject it should be remembered, however, that inter-marriage between the white peoples and the yellow races (the Chinese and the Japanese) is equally un-fortunate and—with the rarest exception—seldom proves successful and is never satisfactory where the children of such unions are concerned. The world war (1914-1945) has itself produced a great admixture of races. Where marching armies go there is inevitable promiscu-ity and a resultant new population; the world today is producing and will produce the results of these (so-called) illicit unions between the soldiers of all nations and the peoples of the countries in which they find themselves. These children of mixed race, as well as the half-castes and the Eurasians may be the answer to a large part of the problem. There will be hundreds of thousands of these children of mixed parentage, forming part of the world population in the next genera-tion and immediate cycle and they are a group with which we will have to reckon.

The Solution

It will be obvious that a finding of a solution to the problem of the minorities is essentially the finding of a solution to the great heresy of separateness. This is immensely difficult not only because of humanity's pre-disposing tendency in this direction, but because that same human nature cannot be easily or rapidly changed. Also, this change and the breaking down of the spirit of separateness has to be brought about in a world of men which is today full of distrust and fear and hardly aware of what is really needed—able only to cry in unison: Give us peace in our time!

If by an act of immediate legislation the Negro minority gained its full rights the problem would remain the same, for the hearts and minds of men would not have been altered and the solution would be entirely superficial; although the Jews have gained their desire and Palestine was handed over to them the anti-Semitic feeling present—with practically no exception—in every nation remains exactly the same as before, plus the bloodshed in Palestine.

The problem goes far deeper than is often estimated; it is inherent in human nature and is the product of countless centuries of fostered growth and the wrong type of education of the masses. Nation is still pitted against nation in the political arena, group against group and (within the nations) party against party and man against man. The wise and the farseeing, those prompted by a sane and unselfish commonsense, the idealist and the men and women of goodwill are everywhere and are struggling to find a solution, to build a new world structure of law, order and peace, which will insure right human relations; but they are, in turn, a tiny minority in comparison to the vast multitude of human beings peopling our earth; their task is hard and from the point at which they must work, appears to them at times as presenting well-nigh insuperable difficulties.

Certain questions inevitably arise in the minds of the men of goodwill everywhere:

Can the Great Powers be trusted to function selflessly in the interests of the Little Powers and of humanity as a whole?

Can power politics and the various national imperialisms be forgotten and ended?

Can a world policy be devised which will insure justice for all whether great or small?

Can world opinion be sufficiently strong in the interests of right human relations that it can tie the hands of the selfishly aggressive and open the door of opportunity to those who have as yet had little?

Is the hope of establishing an era of right human relations within nations as well as internationally, an impossible dream, a waste of time to consider or an evidence only of wishful thinking?

Does the goal of right human relations, equal rights and opportunity for all men everywhere provide an entirely possible goal for which all well-intentioned men can work with some hope of success?

What are the first steps which should be taken to promote such right endeavors and to lay a secure foundation of world goodwill?

How can public opinion be sufficiently aroused so that the many steps to promote right human relations will be faced by legislators and politicians everywhere?

What should the minorities do in order to gain their just demands, without promoting more differences and feeding the fire of hatred?

How can we abolish the great lines of demarcation between races, nations and groups, and the cleavages that are to be found everywhere, working in such a manner that the "one humanity" emerges in the arena of world affairs?

How can we develop the consciousness that what is good for the part can also be good for the whole and that the highest good of the unit within the whole guarantees the good of that whole?

These and many other questions arise and clamor for an answer. The answer comes in the form of a generally accepted platitude and is unfortunately in the nature of an anti-climax: *Establish right human relations by developing a spirit of goodwill.* Then and only then shall we have a world at peace and ready to move forward into a new and better era. Though a platitude is, in the majority of cases, the statement of a recognizable truth, it is difficult in this case to make people admit its feasibility. Nevertheless, because it is a truth, it is bound eventually to demonstrate as such, not only in the minds of a few people here and there but on a large scale throughout the world. People are looking eagerly for the unexpected and the unusual, for an anticipated miracle and for God (whatever they mean in their own minds by that term) to take action, thus relieving them of responsibility and doing their work for them.

Not by such methods do men move forward; not by shifting responsibility do they learn and progress. The miracle may happen and the beautiful and the unexpected appear but only when men have themselves created the right setting and by the wonder of their own achievement made it possible for a still more wonderful expression of rightness to manifest. We can have no further expression of divinity until men act more divinely than at present; we shall have no "return of Christ" or a downpouring of the Christ consciousness until the Christ in every man is more awake and alert than is at present the case; the Prince of Peace or the Spirit of Peace will not make the presence of peace felt on earth until the peaceful intentions of men everywhere are changing the aspect of world affairs. Unity will not be the distinctive characteristic of mankind until men have themselves pulled down the separating walls, and have removed the barriers between race and race, between nation and nation, between religion and religion and between man and man.

The wonder of the present situation and its outstanding opportunity is that for the first time, and on a planetary scale, men are aware of the evil which must be eliminated; everywhere there is discussion and planning; there are meetings and forums, and conferences and committees, ranging all the way from the great deliberations of the United Nations down to the tiny meetings held in some remote village.

The beauty of the present situation is that even in the smallest community a practical expression of what is needed on a worldwide scale is offered to the in-

habitants; differences in families, in churches, in munici-
palities, in cities, in nations, between races and internationally all call for the same objective and for the
same process of adjustment: *the establishing of right
human relations.* The technique or method to bring this
about remains everywhere the same: *the use of the
spirit of goodwill.*

Goodwill is the simplest expression of true love and
the one most easily understood. The use of goodwill in
connection with the problems with which humanity is
faced releases the intelligence along constructive lines;
where goodwill is present, the walls of separation and of
misunderstanding fall.

Love and understanding will eventually follow upon
a practical expression of goodwill as a factor in every
type of human relation and as a mode of contact between groups, between nations and their minorities, between nation and nation and also in the field of
international politics and religions. The expression of
true love as a factor in the life of our planet may lie
very far ahead, but goodwill is a present possibility and
the organizing of goodwill an outstanding necessity.

There is today much talk about goodwill and a constant use of the word; there is a real intention to employ it in every field of human thought and in relation
to every human problem; there is evidence that there is
a real effort at this time to make goodwill an effective
agent in negotiating world peace and understanding and
in bringing about right human relations.

The major need is an immediate campaign, carried
forward by all men of goodwill everywhere throughout
the world to interpret the meaning of goodwill, to emphasize the practical nature of its expression, to gather
together into an effective and active world group all
men and women of goodwill and to do this, not in order
to create a super-organization, but to convince the un-

happy, the distressed and the abused of the magnitude of the intelligent aid which stands ready to assist them. They must also demonstrate their ability to strengthen the hands of all workers who are struggling to bring about right human relations and prove to them the potency of the force of an educated and alive public opinion (educated by the men of goodwill) upon which they can draw. Thus there will be established in every nation, in every city and village, men of goodwill—with trained understanding, practical commonsense, a knowledge of world problems and a willingness to spread goodwill and find the men of like mind in their environment.

The work of the men of goodwill is an educational one. They hold and advocate no miraculous solution of world problems but they *know* that a spirit of goodwill, particularly if trained and implemented by knowledge, can produce *an atmosphere* and *an attitude* which will make the solving of problems possible. When men of goodwill meet, no matter what their political party, nation or religion, there is no problem which they cannot eventually solve and solve to the satisfaction of the various parties involved. *It is the production of this atmosphere and the evocation of this attitude which is the principal work of the men of goodwill and not the presentation of some cut and dried solution.* This spirit of goodwill can be present even where there is fundamental disagreement between parties. But this is seldom the case today. There is a real spirit of goodwill controlling quite a few of the discussions of the United Nations organization on quite difficult and touchy points, and this is becoming increasingly apparent.

There is absolutely no reason to believe that the growth of goodwill in the world need be a slow and gradual affair. The reverse can be the case if the men and women who today feel within themselves a genuine goodwill and who are free from prejudice will seek each other out and work together to spread goodwill. A prejudiced person, a religious fanatic, or a staunch nationalist have a hard task in developing true goodwill within themselves. They can accomplish it if they care enough for their fellowman, and seek to leave him free, but they will have to seek for the dark area in their own minds where a wall of separativeness exists and tear it down. They will have to develop (with deliberation) true goodwill (*not* tolerance) towards the object of their prejudice, towards the man of an alien religion and towards the nation or race to which they feel antagonistic or upon which they look down. A prejudice is a first brick in a separating wall.

Goodwill is far more widespread throughout the world than people think; it simply needs to be discovered, educated and set to work. It must not be exploited, however, by groups working for their own ends, no matter how honestly, correctly or sincerely. It would, if that was done, be diverted into a partisan effort. The men of goodwill stand midway between opposing groups where such exist, in order to create a condition in which discussion and compromise can become happily possible. They tread constantly the "noble middle path" of the Buddha which runs between the pairs of opposites, straight to the very heart of God; they tread the "narrow way" of love of which Christ spoke, and they indicate they are treading it by an expression of the only aspect of love which humanity can at present understand: *Goodwill*.

When goodwill is expressed and organized, recognized and used, world problems, no matter what they may be, will in due time reach solution; when goodwill is a true and active factor in human affairs, we shall then pass on to a fuller and richer understanding of the nature of love and to an expression of some still higher aspect of that divine love; when goodwill is widespread among men, we shall see the establishing of right human relations and a new spirit of confidence, trust and understanding will be found in mankind.

Men and women of goodwill exist in every nation and in all parts of the world in their innumerable thousands. Let these be found, reached and put in touch with each other; let them be set to work to create a right atmosphere in world affairs and in their own communities; let them know that associated they are omnipotent and that they can so educate and train public opinion that the world attitude to world problems will be right and correct and in line with the divine plan; let them realize that the solutions of the critical problems with which humanity is faced at the portal of the New Age will not be found by deciding upon some line of action and forcing it on public attention by propaganda and by campaigning. It will come by advocating and developing a spirit of goodwill (with its results: a right atmosphere and a sound attitude) and an understanding heart.

The Christian era was ushered in by a mere handful of men, the twelve Apostles, the seventy disciples and the five hundred who recognized the message of the Christ. The new era in which Christ will "see of the travail of His soul and be satisfied", is being ushered in by the hundreds of thousands of the men of goodwill now active in the world and who can become still more active if recognized, reached and organized.

CHAPTER V

THE PROBLEM OF THE CHURCHES

THE title of this chapter is not called the problem of religion but simply the problem of those people and organizations who attempt to teach religion, who claim to represent the spiritual life, to direct the spiritual approach of the human soul to God and to lay down the rules for the spiritual life. In writing on this theme we are treading on dangerous ground.

There is no justifiable quarrel with the religious spirit; it exists and is essential to a full and true life on earth. We can recognize the timelessness of faith and the witness of the Spirit, down countless ages, to the *fact of God. Christ lives* and guides the people of the world and He does this not from any vague or distant center called the "right hand of God" (a symbolic phrase), but from close at hand and near to humanity whom He eternally loves. When He said, "Lo, I am with you all the days, even unto the end of the world", He meant exactly what He said. The approach of the human Spirit to its Source, to that spiritual Center where divinity rules and to those Who guide and direct that approach, will inevitably go on; the *way* stands eternally open to pilgrims and all such pilgrims, all souls, find their way eventually into the Father's Home.

The fact of God, the fact of Christ, the fact of men's spiritual approach to divinity, the fact of the deathlessness of the Spirit, the fact of spiritual opportunity and the fact of man's relation to God and to his fellowmen— upon these we can take our stand. We should emphasize also the evolutionary presentation of truth and its constant adaptation to the need of humanity at any given period in history.

Christianity is an expression—in essence, if not yet factually—of the love of God, immanent in His created universe. Churchianity has, however, laid itself open to attack and the mass of thinking people know this; unfortunately, these thinking people are a small minority.

For the sake of clarity and in order that the outline of the facts and of the potentialities may emerge clearly, we will divide this subject into the following sections, beginning with the most unpleasant and controversial and ending on a note of hope, of purpose and of vision.

I. The Failure of the Churches. Would you, in all truthfulness and in the light of world events, say that the churches had succeeded?

II. The Opportunity of the Churches. Do they recognize it?

III. The Essential Truths which Humanity needs and intuitively accepts. What are they?

IV. The Regeneration of the Churches. Is it possible?

V. The New World Religion.

Today the immediate need of mankind is emerging with clarity, and the steps which the churches propose taking to meet that need are also becoming clear. It seems essential, therefore, that we face the situation exactly as it is and that we isolate those truths which are essential to man's progress and enlightenment and eliminate factors which are controversial and unimportant; it is necessary also that we define the way of salvation which the churches should follow; if the churches are working and the churchmen are thinking in a Christlike way, then the salvation of humanity is assured. It is above all else essential that a vision is presented which will be a vision for all men everywhere and not simply a beautiful hope of a sectarian group or a fanatical self-satisfied organization. It is essential that we return to Christ and to His message and to the way of life exemplified by Him.

Churchmen need to remember that the human spirit is greater than the churches and greater than their teaching. In the long run, that human spirit will defeat them and proceed triumphantly into the kingdom of God, leaving them far behind unless they enter as an humble part of the mass of men. Pompous prelates and executive ecclesiastics have no part in that kingdom. Christ does not need prelates and executives. He needs humble teachers of the truth able to exemplify the spiritual life. Nothing under heaven can arrest the progress of the human soul on its long pilgrimage from darkness to light, from the unreal to the real, from death to immortality and from ignorance to wisdom. If the great organized religious groups of churches in every land and composing all faiths do not offer *spiritual* guidance and help, humanity will find another way. Nothing can keep the spirit of man from God.

I. THE FAILURE OF THE CHURCHES

Let us remember: *Christ has not failed.* It is the human element which has failed and which has thwarted His intentions, and prostituted the truth which He presented. Theology, dogma, doctrine, materialism, politics and money have created a vast dark cloud between the churches and God; they have shut out the true vision of God's love, and it is to this vision of a loving reality and to a vital recognition of its implications that we must return.

Is there any chance that a renewal of the faith as it was in Christ will return? Are there enough men of vision in the churches to save the day—a vision of meeting the need of man and not a vision of the growth and aggrandizement of the churches? Such men *do exist* in every religious organization, but they are deplorably few. Even if united (which seems as yet sadly impossible because of doctrinal differences), they present a somewhat futile group versus the organized power, the materialistic splendor, the vested interests and the fanatical determination of the reactionary ecclesiastics of all faiths. It is usually the struggling minority (in this case the spiritually-minded few) who guard the true vision and finally bring it into being; they are the ones who walk the torrid, unhappy streets with agonizing humanity and who, therefore, recognize in an acute sense the need for the regeneration of the churches.

Our religious platforms, our pulpits, and our religious periodicals and magazines are full of appeals for men to turn again to God and to find in religion a way out of the present chaotic conditions. Yet, humanity has never before been so spiritually inclined or so consciously and definitely oriented to the spiritual values and to the need for spiritual revaluations and realizations. The appeals going out should be made to the church leaders and to the ecclesiastics of all faiths and to church workers everywhere; it is *they* who should return to the simplicity of the faith as it is in Christ. It is *they* who need regeneration. Men are everywhere demanding light. Who is to give it to them?

There are two major factors which are responsible for the failure of the churches:

1. Narrow theological interpretations of the Scriptures.

2. Material and political ambitions.

In every land down the ages men have sought to foist their personal, religious interpretations of truth, of the Scriptures and of God upon the mass of men. They have taken the Bibles of the world and have attempted to explain them, passing the ideas they find through the filter of their own minds and brains and in the process inevitably stepping down the meaning. Not content with this, their followers have forced these man-evolved interpretations upon the unthinking and the ignorant. Every religion—Buddhism, Hinduism in its many aspects, Mohammedanism and Christianity—has produced a flock of outstanding minds who have sought (usually quite sincerely) to understand what God is supposed to have said, who have formulated doctrines and dogmas on this basis of what they thought God meant and their words and ideas have, therefore, become religious law and the irrefutable truths of countless millions. In the last analysis, what have you? The ideas of some human mind—interpreted in terms of his period, tradition and background—about what God said in some Scripture which has been subjected during the centuries to the difficulties and the mistakes incident to constant translation—a translation often based on oral teaching.

The doctrine of the verbal inspiration of the Scriptures of the world (deemed particularly applicable to the Christian Bible) is today completely exploded and with it the infallibility of interpretation; all the world Scriptures are now seen to be based on poor translations and no part of them—after thousands of years of translation—is as it originally was, if it ever existed as an original manuscript and was not in reality some man's recollection of what was said. At the same time, it must be remembered that the general trend and the basic teaching, as well as the significance of the symbols, is usually correct, though again, symbolism itself must be subjected to modern translation and not to the misinterpretation of ignorance. The point is that dogmas and doctrines, theology and dogmatic affirmations, do not necessarily indicate the truth as it exists in the mind of God, with Whose mind the majority of dogmatic interpreters claim familiarity. Theology is simply what men *think* is in the mind of God.

The more ancient the Scripture, the greater, necessarily, the distortion. The doctrine of a vengeful God, the doctrine of retribution in some mythical hell, the teaching that God only loves those who interpret Him in terms of some particular school of theological thought, the symbolism of the blood sacrifice, the appropriation of the Cross as a Christian symbol, the teaching about the Virgin Birth and the picture of an angry Deity only appeased by death are the unhappy results of man's own thinking, of his own lower nature, of his sectarian isolationism (fostered by the Jewish *Old Testament,* but not generally found in the Oriental faiths) and of his sense of fear, inherited from the animal side of his nature—all these are fostered and inculcated by theology but not by Christ, or the Buddha or Shri Krishna.

The little minds of men at their past and present stages of evolution cannot today and never have comprehended the mind and the purposes of the One in Whom we live and move and have our being; they have interpreted God in terms of themselves; therefore when men unthinkingly accept a dogma, they are only accepting the point of view of some other fallible human being, and are not accepting a divine truth at all. It is this truth that theological seminaries must begin to teach, training their men to think for themselves and to remember that the key to truth lies in the unifying power of Comparative Religion. Only those principles and truths which are universally recognized and which find their place in every religion are truly necessary to salvation. The secondary and controversial line of presented truths is usually unnecessary or significant only in so far as it buttresses the primary and essential truth.

It is this distorted presentation of truth which has led humanity to the formulation of a body of doctrines about which Christ apparently knew nothing. Christ cared only that men should recognize that God is love, that all men are the children of the one Father and, therefore, brothers; that man's spirit is eternal and that there is no death; He longed that the Christ within every man (the innate Christ consciousness which makes us one with each other and with Christ) should flower forth in all its glory; He taught that service was the keynote of the spiritual life and that the will of God would be revealed. These are *not* the points about which the mass of commentators have written. They have discussed ad nauseam how far Christ was divine and how far He was human, the nature of the Virgin Birth, the function of St. Paul as a teacher of Christian truth, the nature of hell, salvation through blood, and the authenticity and historicity of the Bible.

Today men's minds are recognizing the dawn of freedom; they are realizing that every man should be free to worship God in his own way. This will not mean (in the coming new age) that every man will pick a theological school to which he will choose to adhere. His own God-illumined mind will search for truth and he will interpret it for himself. The day of theology is over and that of a living truth is with us. This the orthodox churches refuse to recognize. Truth is essentially non-controversial; where controversy emerges, the concept is usually secondary in importance and consists largely of men's ideas about truth.

Men have gone far today in the rejection of dogmas and doctrine and this is good and right and encouraging. It signifies progress, but, as yet, the churches fail to see in this the workings of divinity. Freedom of thought, the questioning of presented truths, a refusal to accept the teachings of the churches in terms of the past theology, and a rejection of imposed ecclesiastical authority are characteristic of creative spiritual thinking at this time; this is regarded by orthodox churchmen as indicative of dangerous tendencies and as a turning away from God and, consequently, of a loss of the sense of divinity. *It indicates exactly the reverse.*

Perhaps as serious, because of its effect upon untold thousands of the more ignorant public, are the materialistic and political ambitions of the churches. In the Eastern faiths this is not so prominently the case; in the Western world this tendency is fast bringing on the degeneration of the churches. In the Oriental religions a disastrous negativity has prevailed; the truths given out have not sufficed to better the daily life of the believer or to anchor the truths creatively upon the physical plane. The effect of the Eastern doctrines is largely subjective and negative as to daily affairs. The negativity of the theological interpretations of the Buddhist and Hindu Scriptures have kept the people in a quiescent condition from which they are slowly beginning to emerge. The Mohammedan faith is, like the Christian, a positive presentation of truth though very materialistic; both these faiths have been militant and political in their activities.

The great Western faith, Christianity, has been definitely objective in its presentation of truth; this was needed. It has been militant, fanatical, grossly materialistic and ambitious. It has combined political objectives with pomp and ceremony, with great stone structures, with power and an imposed authority of a most cramping nature.

The early Christian Church (which was relatively pure in its presentation of truth and in its living processes) eventually split into three main divisions—

the Roman Catholic Church which today seeks to make capital out of the claim that it was the Mother Church, the Byzantine or Greek Orthodox Church and the Protestant Churches. All of them split away on the question of doctrine and all of them were originally sincere and clean and relatively pure and good. All have steadily deteriorated since the day of their inception and today the following sad and serious situation can be found:

1. *The Roman Catholic Church* is distinguished by three things which are all contrary to the spirit of Christ:

a. An intensely materialistic attitude. The Church of Rome stands for great stone structures—cathedrals, churches, institutions, convents, monasteries. In order to build them, the policy down the centuries has been to drain the money out of the pockets of rich and poor alike. The Roman Catholic Church is a strictly capitalistic church. The money gathered into its coffers supports a powerful ecclesiastical hierarchy and provides for its many institutions and schools.

b. A far-reaching and far-sighted political program in which temporal power is the goal and not the welfare of the little people. The present program of the Catholic Church has definite political implications; their attitude to Communism has in it the seeds of another world war. The political activities of the Catholic Church have not built for peace, no matter under what guise they are presented.

c. A planned policy whereby the mass of the people are kept in intellectual ignorance and, through this ignorance, are naturally to be found among the reactionary and conservative forces which are so powerfully at work resisting the new age with its new civilization and more enlightened culture. Blind faith and complete confidence in the priest and in the Vatican are regarded as spiritual duties.

The Roman Catholic Church stands entrenched and unified against any new and evolutionary presentation of truth to the people; its roots are in the past but it is not growing into the light; its vast financial resources enable it to menace the future enlightenment of mankind under the cloak of paternalism and a colorful outer appearance which hides a crystallization and an intellectual stupidity which must inevitably spell its eventual doom, unless the faint stirrings of new life following the advent of Pope John XXIII can be nourished and developed.

2. *The Greek Orthodox Church* reached such a high stage of corruption, graft, greed and sexual evil that, temporarily and under the Russian revolution, it was abolished. This was a wise, needed and right action. The emphasis of this church was entirely material but it never wielded (nor will it wield) such power as the Roman Catholic Church did in the past. The refusal of the revolutionary party in Russia to recognize this corrupt church was wise and salutary; it did no harm, for the sense of God can never be driven from the human heart. If all church organizations disappeared from off the earth, the sense of God and the recognition and the knowledge of Christ would emerge in strength and with a fresh and new conviction. The church in Russia has again received official recognition and faces a new opportunity. It does not yet constitute a factor in world affairs but there is hope that eventually it may emerge as a regenerating and spiritual force. The challenge of its environment is great and it cannot be reactionary as can—and are—the churches in other parts of the world.

3. *The Protestant Churches*. The church, covered by the generic name of "protestant", is distinguished by its multiplicity of divisions; it is broad, narrow, liberal, radical and ever protesting.   It comprises within its borders many churches, large and small. These churches are also distinguished by material objectives. They are relatively free from any such political bias as conditions the Roman Catholic Church, but it is a quarreling, fanatical and intolerant body of believers. The spirit of differentiation is rampant; there is no unity or cohesion among them, but usually a constant spirit of rejection, a virulent partisanship and the growth of hundreds of protestant cults, a constant presentation of a narrow theology which teaches nothing new but produces fresh quarreling around some doctrines or some question of church organization or procedure. The Protestant Churches have set a precedent of acrimonious controversy from which the older churches are relatively free, owing to their hierarchical method of government and their centralized authoritarian control. Again, however, the first efforts to achieve some form of unity and cooperation have recently emerged and may continue to grow.

The question arises whether Christ would be at home in the churches if He walked again among men. The rituals and the ceremonies, the pomp and the vestments, the candles and the gold and silver, the graded order of popes, cardinals, archbishops, canons and ordinary rectors, pastors and clergy would seemingly have small interest to the simple Son of God Who— when on earth—had nowhere to lay His head.

There are deeply spiritual men whose lot is cast within the cramping walls of ecclesiasticism; they are many in the aggregate, and within all churches and faiths. Their lot is a difficult one; they are aware of conditions and they struggle and strive to present sound

Christian and religious ideas to a searching, suffering world. They are true sons of God; their feet are set in most unpleasant places; they are aware of the "dry rot" which has undermined the clerical structure and of the bigotry, selfishness, greed and narrow-mindedness with which they are surrounded.

They know well that *no man has ever been saved by theology but only by the living Christ and through the awakened consciousness of the Christ within each human heart;* they interiorly repudiate the materialism in their environment and see little hope for humanity in the churches; they know well that the spiritual realities have been forgotten in the material development of the churches; they love their fellowmen and would like to divert the money spent in the upkeep of church structures and overhead to the creation of that Temple of God "not made with hands, eternal in the heavens". They serve that spiritual Hierarchy which stands—unseen and serene—behind all human affairs and feel no inner allegiance to any outer ecclesiastical hierarchy. The guidance of the human being into conscious relation to Christ and that spiritual Hierarchy is to them the factor of major importance and not the increase of church attendance and the authority of little men. They believe in the Kingdom of God of which Christ is the outstanding Executive but have no confidence in the temporal power claimed and wielded by Popes and Archbishops.

Such men are found in every great religious organization, both in the East and in the West and in all spiritual groups, dedicated ostensibly to spiritual purpose. They are simple, saintly men, asking nothing for the separated self, representing God in truth and in life, and having no real part in the church wherein they work; the church suffers sadly through the contrast which they represent and seldom permits them to rise to place and power; their temporal power is nil but their spiritual example brings illumination and strength to their people. They are the hope of humanity for they are in touch with Christ and are an integral part of the Kingdom of God; they represent Deity in a manner which the great ecclesiastics and the so-called Princes of the Church seldom do.

II. THE OPPORTUNITY OF THE CHURCHES

Something of great moment has happened in the world. The spirit of destruction has stampeded through the earth, leaving the world of the past and the civilization which controlled our modern life in ruins. Cities and homes have been destroyed; kingdoms and rulers have disappeared in the aftermath of war; ideologies and cherished beliefs have failed to meet the need of people and have broken down under the test of the times; starvation and insecurity are rampant everywhere; families and social groups have been disrupted; death has taken its toll of every nation and millions have died as a result of the inhuman processes of war. Broadly speaking, everyone has known terror, fear and hopelessness as they face the future; everyone is questioning what that future has in store and there is no surety anywhere. The voice of humanity is demanding light, peace and security.

Some seek it in the formation of new ideologies; some look for it along political lines and hope for relief and release through some form of government action or some political creed or party. Others demand the emergence of a leader, and there are few leaders anywhere to be seen at this time. The leadership provided is coming from groups of well-meaning people and a few statesmen who seem as bewildered as those they seek to help; they are rendered well-nigh impotent by the very magnitude of the task with which they are faced, for the issue at stake is the rebuilding, the reconditioning and the re-educating of the entire world. Still others, more patient, are planning new educational processes and systems which will attempt to prepare the present generation of children for full living in the world of tomorrow, a world whose faint outlines are only dimly to be seen. Some are sinking back into a state of despair, escaping into isolationism and waiting, as philosophically as possible, for the release which death will bring, asking only a little food, some warmth, a few books and sufficient clothing. Many are refusing altogether to think and are instead filling their lives with relief work. All are experiencing the reaction which follows in the aftermath of war and are not familiar with the processes of peace, because peace has never truly been known and is obviously still far away.

Above everything else, men throughout the world in their countless millions are registering a deep spiritual need, are conscious of the stirrings of the spirit and are recognizing it for what it is. They may express this need in many forms and use many differing terminologies; they may look in diverse directions for the satisfaction of their longings, but everywhere there *is* a demand for things of truer value than those which conditioned the past and for the appearance of those virtues, spiritual impulses and incentives which men appear to have lost and which are the sum total of the forces which drive humanity on towards spiritual living.

Everywhere people are ready for the light; they are expectant of a new revelation and of a new dispensation. Humanity has advanced so far on the way of evolution that these demands and expectations are not couched in terms óf material betterment only, but in terms of a spiritual vision, true values and right human relations. They are demanding teaching and spiritual help along with the necessary requests for food, clothes and the opportunity to work and live in freedom; they face famine in large areas of the world and yet are registering with equal dismay the famine of the soul.

The great tragedy is, however, that they know not where to turn or to whose voice they should listen. The hope within them is spiritual and undying. This hope and this demand have reached the attentive ear of the Christ and His disciples in the place where They live, and work and watch over humanity. Through what agency will these forces of the spirit work for the restoration of the world? By what means will the spiritual Guides of the race lead men forward into greater light and the opportunity of the new age? Mankind faces towards the Way of Resurrection. Who shall lead him on that Way?

Will the organized religions and the churches throughout the world recognize the opportunity and respond to the appeal of Christ and to the spiritual demand of countless millions? Or will they work for organizations and the churches? Will the institutional aspect of the world religions loom more largely in the consciousness of churchmen than the need of the people for a simple presentation of life-giving truth? Will the interest and the power of the churches be turned to the rebuilding of the material structures, the re-establishing of financial security, the recovery of the status of outgrown theologies and the attainment anew of temporal power and prestige? Or will the churches have the vision and the courage to let the bad old ways go and turn to the people with the message that God is Love, proving the existence of that love by their own lives of simple loving service? Will they tell the people that Christ forever lives and bid them turn their eyes away from the old doctrines of death and blood and divine appeasement and center them upon the Source of all life and upon the living Christ Who waits to pour out upon them that "life more abundantly" for which they have so long waited and which He promised should be theirs? Will they teach that the destruction of the old forms was needed and that their disappearence is the guarantee that a new and fuller unlimited spiritual life is now possible? Will they remind the people that Christ Himself said that it is not possible to put new wine into old bottles? Will the potentates of the churches and the proud ecclesiastics relinquish publicly their wrong and material aims, their money and their palaces and "sell all that they have" and follow Christ on the path of service? Or will they—like the rich young man in the Gospel story—turn sadly away? Will they spend the available money in alleviating pain as Christ did, teaching the children the things of the kingdom of God as Christ did, and setting an example of simple faith, confident joy and assured knowledge of God as Christ did? Can churchmen of all faiths in both hemispheres attain that inner spiritual light which will make them light bearers and which will evoke that greater light which the new and anticipated revelation will surely bring? Can the materialism for which the churches have stood and the failures of their representatives to teach the people aright be swept away? These were the things which were responsible for the world war (1914-1945). There could have been no war if greed, hate and separativeness had not been rampant upon the earth and in the hearts of men; these disastrous faults were there because the spiritual values had no place in the life of the people and this was due to the fact that for centuries they have had small place in the life of the churches. The responsibility rests squarely upon the churches.

These are the questions with which the organized churches are confronted. Within the churches today there are men responding to the new spiritual idealism,

to the urgency of the opportunity and to the need for
change. But the opportunity is controlled by reactionary
minds. The movements towards the reorganization of the
churches which are now proceeding all over the world
still remain in the hands of the church dignitaries and
synods and conclaves. The plans internationally being
formed at this time would indicate that the authority is
still vested in the wrong people.

There is no indication on any large scale within the
churches of a basic change of attitude towards theological teaching or church government. There is no indication that the great Oriental religions are taking an
active lead in producing a new and better world. And
still humanity waits. Humanity wants above all else
assurance that God Is and that there is a divine Plan—a
Plan which fits into the scheme of things and which
holds within it both hope and strength. Men want the
conviction that Christ lives; that the Coming One—for
Whom all men wait—will come and that He will not
be Christian, Hindu or Buddhist *but will belong to all
men everywhere*. Men want to be assured that a great
spiritual revelation is due and cannot be arrested and
that there lies ahead of them a spiritual future as well
as a material one. It is with this demand and this opportunity that the churches are faced.

What is the solution of this intricate and difficult
relationship throughout the world? A new presentation
of truth, because God is not a fundamentalist; a new
approach to divinity, because God is ever accessible and
requires no outer intermediaries today; a new mode of
interpreting the ancient spiritual teaching, because man
has evolved and what was suitable for infant humanity
is today unsuitable for adult mankind. These are im-
perative changes.

Nothing can prevent the new world religion from
eventually emerging. It always has down the ages and

it always will. There is no finality in the presentation of truth; it develops and grows to meet man's growing demand for light. It will be implemented and developed by the spiritually minded in all churches, whose minds are open to the new inspirations of God's Mind, who are liberal and kind and whose individual lives are pure and aspiring. It will be hindered by the fundamentalists, the narrow-minded and the theologians in all the world religions, by those who refuse to let go the old interpretations and methods, who love the old doctrines and men's thoughts about them, and by those who lay the emphasis upon forms, upon rites and ceremonies, upon ritual and pomp, on authority and the building of stone edifices in these days of man's extremity, his starvation and his need.

The Roman Catholic Church here faces her greatest opportunity and also her greatest crisis. Catholicism is founded in ancient tradition, is assertive of ecclesiastical authority, is responsive to outer forms and rituals and—in spite of a wide and beneficent philanthropy—is quite unable to leave her children free. If the Catholic Church can change her techniques, can relinquish authority over the souls of men (which she has never truly had) and can really follow the way of the Saviour, of the humble Carpenter of Nazareth, she can render a world service and set an example which will serve to enlighten the followers of every faith and of every branch of Christianity.

The problem of the freedom of the human soul and its *individual* relation to God Immanent and God Transcendent is the spiritual problem, facing all the world religions at this time. No longer must the churches interpose their authority and their interpretations between God and man. The time for that is past. This problem has been slowly shaping up for centuries, developing with the growth of the human intellect and the self-consciousness of the human being and it is one which now cries aloud for solution.

III. THE ESSENTIAL TRUTHS

There are certain keynotes—embodying the future of religion—which should govern the thinking of enlightened churchmen of all faiths at this time. They are appropriate to both the East and the West. These are: World Religion—Revelation—Recognition. They will not be accepted by the narrow-minded Christian or believer of any faith.

The day is dawning when all religions will be regarded as emanating from one great spiritual source; all will be seen as unitedly providing the one root out of which the universal world religion will inevitably emerge. Then there will be neither Christian nor heathen, neither Jew nor Gentile, but simply one great body of believers, gathered out of all the current religions. They will accept the same truths, not as theological concepts but as essential to spiritual living; they will stand together on the same platform of brotherhood and of human relations; they will recognize divine sonship and will seek unitedly to cooperate with the divine Plan, as it is revealed to them by the spiritual leaders of the race, and as it indicates to them the next step to be taken on the Path of Approach to God. Such a *world religion* is no idle dream but something which is definitely forming today.

A second emerging guide to the spiritual life is the hope of *revelation*. Never before has man's need been greater and never has the surety of revelation been more certain; never has the spirit of man been more invocative of divine aid than it is today and, therefore, never before has a greater revelation been on its way. What that revelation will be, we cannot know. The revelation of the nature of God has been a slow unfolding process, paralleled by the evolutionary growth of the human consciousness. It is not for us to define or limit it with our concrete thinking but to prepare for it, to unfold our intuitive perception and to live in expectation of the revealing light.

A *world religion,* an expected *revelation* and then the development of the habit of *spiritual recognition!* It is the task of the churches to teach men to unfold this latent power of recognition—recognition of the beauty of divinity in all forms, recognition of that which is coming and of what an old Hindu seer has spoken of as the "raincloud of knowable things" which hovers over humanity, ready to precipitate the wonders which God holds in store for those who know the meaning of love. It is along these three lines that the work of the churches should, in the future, be directed; the carrying forward of this task would truly restore the churches and obliterate all the failures of the past.

In these three attitudes there are certain basic truths which the churches can present to men everywhere— truths which are uniform in all the world religions:

1. *The Fact of God, Immanent and Transcendent*

The Eastern faiths have ever emphasized God immanent, deep within the human heart, "nearer than hands or feet", the Self, the One, the Atma, smaller than the small, yet all-comprehensive. The Western faiths have presented God transcendent, outside His universe, an Onlooker. God transcendent first of all conditioned men's concept of Deity, for the action of this transcendent God appeared in the processes of nature; later, in the Jewish dispensation, God appeared as the tribal Jehovah, as the soul (the rather unpleasant soul) of a nation. Next God was seen as a perfected man, and the divine God-man walked the earth in the Person of Christ. Today we have a rapidly growing emphasis upon God immanent in every human being and in every created form. Today we should have the churches presenting a synthesis of these two ideas which have been summed up for us in the statement of Shri Krishna in the *Bhagavad Gita:* "Having pervaded this whole universe with a fragment of Myself, I remain". God, greater than the created whole, yet God present also in the part; God transcendent guarantees the plan for our world and is the Purpose, conditioning all lives from the minutest atom, up through all the kingdoms of nature to man.

2. *The Fact of Immortality and Eternal Persistence*

The spirit in man is undying; it forever endures, progressing from point to point and stage to stage upon the Path of Evolution, unfolding steadily and sequentially the divine attributes and aspects. This truth involves necessarily the recognition of two great natural laws: the Law of Rebirth and the Law of Cause and Effect. The churches in the West have refused officially to recognize the Law of Rebirth and have thereby wandered into a theological impasse and into a cul-de-sac from which there is no possible exit. The churches in the East have overemphasized these laws so that a negative, acquiescent attitude to life and its processes, based on continuously renewed opportunity, controls the people. Christianity has emphasized immortality but has made eternal happiness dependent upon the acceptance of a theological dogma: Be a true professing Christian and live eternally in a somewhat fatuous heaven or refuse to be an accepting Christian and go to an impossible hell —a hell growing out of the theology of *The Old Testament* and its presentation of a God full of hate and jealousy. Both concepts are today repudiated by all sane, sincere, thinking people. No one of any true reasoning power or with any true belief in a God of love accepts the heaven of the churchmen or has any desire to go there. Still less do they accept the "lake that burneth with fire and brimstone" or the everlasting torture to which a God of love is supposed to condemn all who do not believe in the theological interpretations of the Middle Ages, of the modern fundamentalists or of the churchmen who seek—through doctrine, fear and threat—to keep people in line with the obsolete old teaching.

The essential truth lies elsewhere. "Whatsoever a man soweth that shall he also reap" is the truth which needs re-emphasizing. In these words, St. Paul phrases for us the ancient and true teaching of the Law of Cause and Effect called in the Orient, the Law of Karma. To that, he adds in another place the injunction to "work out your own salvation" and—as that contradicts the theological teaching and above all else is not possible to do in any one life—he implicitly endorses the Law of Rebirth, and makes the school of life a constantly recurring experience until man has fulfilled the command of the Christ (and this refers to every man) "Be ye, therefore, perfect, even as your Father in Heaven is perfect". Through recognition of the results of action—good or bad—and through constant reliving upon the earth, man eventually attains "unto the measure of the stature of the fulness of the Christ".

The fact of this innate divinity explains the urge at the heart of every man for betterment, for experience, for progress, for increasing realization and for his steady moving on towards the distant height which he has visioned. There is no other explanation of the capacity of the human spirit to emerge out of darkness, out of evil and death into life and goodness. This emergence has been the unfailing history of man. Something is always happening to the human soul which projects him nearer to the Source of all good and nothing on earth can arrest this progress nearer to God.

3. *Christ and the Hierarchy*

The third great spiritual and essential truth is the *fact* of Christ, the living Christ, present among His people, fulfilling His promise, "Lo, I am with you always, even unto the end of the world", and increasingly making His presence felt as men approach closer to Him and His group of disciples and world workers. The church emphasis has been (and is today) upon the dead Christ. Men have forgotten that He lives, though they give a tentative recognition to this hope and belief at Easter time, largely because His resurrection guarantees our own "rising again", and "because He lives, we shall live also". The fact of His livingness and of His presence today, here and now, on earth is not emphasized, except through vague and hopeful generalities. Men have forgotten the Christ who lives with us on earth, surrounded by His disciples, the Masters of the Wisdom, accessible to those who make the right approach and saving men by the force of His example and by the expression of the life which is in Him and is— unexpressed and largely undiscovered as yet by the majority—to be found also in every man.

In the coming world religion, the emphasis will be on these truths. Life and not death will be proclaimed; attainment of spiritual status through spiritual living will be taught, and the fact of the existence of those who have thus attained and who work with Christ for the helping and salvaging of humanity will be the goal. The fact of the spiritual Hierarchy of our planet, the ability of mankind to contact its Members and to work in cooperation with Them, and the existence of Those Who know what the will of God is and can work intelligently with that will—these are the truths upon which the future spiritual teaching will be based.

The fact of the existence of this Hierarchy and its supreme Head, the Christ, is consciously recognized by hundreds of thousands today, though still denied by the orthodox. So many *know* this truth and so many people of integrity and worth are cooperating *consciously* with the Members of the Hierarchy that ecclesiastical antagonisms and the belittling comments of the concrete minded are of no avail. Men are moving out from under doctrinal authority into direct, personal and spiritual experience; they are coming under the direct authority which contact with Christ and His disciples, the Masters, ever confers.

Christ in every man, the guarantee of our eventual spiritual attainment; Christ as the living example of that attainment, Who has entered for us within the veil, leaving us an example that we should follow His steps; Christ Who ever lives and Who has stayed with us for two thousand years, watching over His people, inspiring His working disciples, the Masters of the Wisdom, those "just men, made perfect" (as the Bible calls them); Christ demonstrating for us the possibility of this unfolding, living, spiritual consciousness (which has been given the somewhat vague name of the "Christ consciousness") bringing every man, eventually—under the Laws of Rebirth and of Cause and Effect—to an ultimate perfection; these are the truths which the church will eventually endorse, teach and express through the lives and words of its exponents. This change in the doctrinal presentation will lead to a very different humanity to that which exists today; it will produce a humanity which will recognize the divine in all men, at varying stages of expression, a humanity which is not only expectant of the return of Christ but is assured of His coming and reappearance—not from some distant Heaven but from that place on earth where He has always been, known and reached by thousands but held at a distance by the theologies and the fear-tactics of the church.

His coming will not be so much a triumphant return to a conquering church (conquering because the churches have done so fine a piece of work) but a recognition of His factual existence by those who have hitherto been blind to His presence with them and to the fact of His office and activities, ceaselessly carried forward on earth. He does not return to rule, for He has never left off ruling, working and loving; but men will come to recognize the signs of His activities and of His presence and will know that it is He Who is over-throwing the churches by the strength of His influence over the hearts and lives of men. Men will then realize that the word "spiritual" has little reference to religion, as was hitherto its major significance, but that it con-notes divine activity in every phase of human living and human thinking; they will grasp the stupendous truth that sound economics, clear humanitarianism, effective education (as it fits men for world citizenship) and a science, dedicated to human betterment, are all deeply spiritual and in their aggregated usefulness constitute a body of religious truth; they will discover that organized religion is only one phase of this *worldwide experience of divinity.*

Christ will, therefore, surely come in three ways. He will come as men recognize that He is truly here as He has been ever since He *apparently* left the earth; He will come in the sense also that He will overshadow, inspire and directly guide and personally confer with His advanced disciples as they labor in the field of the world, in the effort to establish right human relations and as they become known as the directing Agents of

God's will; He will come also in the hearts of men everywhere, manifesting as the indwelling Christ, struggling towards the light and influencing the lives of men towards conscious recognition of divinity. Men on a large scale will then pass through the Bethlehem experience, the Christ in them will come to the birth and they will become "new men".

It will be for the dissemination of these *existing* truths that the church of the future will work, bringing a great regeneration to the body of humanity, a resurrection into life, and the restoration of the life of God on earth through a Christ-conscious humanity.

When this has assumed large proportions and the recognition of these truths is worldwide, then we shall have the restoration of the Mysteries, the consequent realization that the Kingdom of God *is* on earth, and that man is in deed and in truth made in the image of God and must inevitably—through the passing of time and the discipline of life—manifest his essential divinity, as Christ did.

4. *The Brotherhood of Man*

Much has been written, preached and talked about brotherhood. So much has been said and so little brotherhood practised that the word has fallen somewhat into disrepute. Yet the word *is* a statement of the underlying origin and goal of humanity and is the keynote of the fourth kingdom in nature, the human.

Brotherhood is a great natural fact; all men are brothers; under the divergences of color, creed, cultures and civilizations, there is only *one* humanity without distinction or differences in its essential nature, in its origin, its spiritual and mental objectives, its capacities, its qualities and its mode of development and of evolutionary unfoldment. In these divine attributes (for that is

what they are) all men are equal; it is only in relation
to time and in the extent to which progress has been
made in the revelation of innate divinity in all its fullness
that temporary differences become apparent. It is the
temporary differences and the sins which ignorance and
inexperience betray which have engrossed the attention
of the churches to the exclusion of the penetrating,
piercing vision of the divine in every man. It is the fact
of brotherhood which the churches must begin to teach
—not from the angle of a transcendent God, an ex-
ternal unknowable Father—but from the angle of the
divine life, eternally present in every human heart, and
eternally struggling to express itself through individuals,
nations and races.

The true expression of this realized brotherhood
must inevitably come through the establishing of right
human relations and the cultivation of goodwill. Churchmen have forgotten the sequence in the angel's song:
"Glory to God in the highest, on earth peace, goodwill
towards men". They have failed to realize and, therefore,
to teach that only as goodwill is manifested in the daily
lives of men are right human relations thereby established and peace on earth can come; they have failed
also to realize that there is no glory to God until there
is peace on earth through goodwill among men. The
churches have forgotten that all men are sons of the
Father and, therefore, brothers; that all men are divine,
that some men are already God-conscious and expressing divinity and that some are not; they have overlooked
the fact that because of their point in evolution some
men know Christ, because the Christ in them is active
while others are only struggling to bring the Christ life
into activity; still others are entirely unaware of the
divine Being hidden deep within their hearts. There
is only difference in degree of consciousness; there is no
difference in nature.

5. *The Divine Approaches*

To all these above truths, essential to human unfoldment, must be added another. This truth is only as yet dimly sensed because it is a larger truth than any hitherto presented to the consciousness of mankind. It is larger because it is related to the Whole and not to individual man alone and his personal salvation. It is an extension of the individual approach to truth. Let us call it the truth concerning the great *Cyclic Approaches* of the divine to the human; of these all world Saviours and Teachers are the symbol and the guarantee. At certain great moments down the ages, God drew nearer to His people and humanity at the same time made great, though oft unconscious efforts to draw near to God. From one angle, it might be regarded as God transcendent recognizing God immanent, and God in man reaching out to God in the Whole and greater than the Whole. On the part of God, working through the Head of the spiritual Hierarchy and its Membership, this effort was intentional, conscious and deliberate; on the part of man, it has been in the past largely unconscious, forced upon humanity by the tragedy of circumstances, by desperate need and by the driving urge of the immanent Christ consciousness.

These great Approaches can be traced down the centuries; each time one took place, it meant a clearer understanding of divine purpose, a new and fresh revelation of divine quality, the institution of some aspect of a new world faith and the sounding of a note which produced a new civilization and culture or a fresh recognition of relationship between God and man or man and his brother.

Back in the dim past of history (hinted at through symbolism and in the Bibles of the world) there was a first major Approach when God took notice of man and something happened—under the action and will of God the Creator, God transcendent—which affected primeval man, and he "became a *living soul*". As the yearning urge towards an undefined and unrealized good made itself felt in the inchoate longings of unthinking man (literally unthinking at that stage), it evoked a response from Deity; God drew near to man and man became imbued with that life and energy which, as time went by, would enable him to recognize himself as a son of God and eventually to express that sonship perfectly. This Approach was signalized by the appearance of the faculty of mind in man. In man was planted the embryonic power to think, to reason and to *know*. The universal Mind of God was reflected in the tiny mind of man.

Later, we are told, when the mental powers of the early humanity warranted it, another Approach between God and man, between the spiritual Hierarchy and humanity, became possible and the door into the Kingdom of God was opened. Man learned that the way into the Holy Place could be entered through *love*. To the mental principle was added—again by the force of invocation and responsive evocation—another divine attribute or principle, the principle of love.

These two great Approaches made it possible for the human soul to express or manifest two aspects of divinity: Intelligence and Love. Intelligence today is flowering through knowledge and science; it has, however, not yet unfolded on any large scale its latent beauty of wisdom; love today is only just beginning to engross human attention; its lowest aspect, *Goodwill*, is only now being recognized as a divine energy and is still a theory and a hope.

The Buddha came embodying in Himself the divine quality of wisdom; He was the manifestation of Light, and the Teacher of the way of enlightenment.   He demonstrated in Himself the processes of illumination and became "the Illumined One". Light, wisdom, reason, as divine yet human attributes, were focussed in the Buddha. He challenged the people to tread the Path of Illumination of which wisdom, mental perception and the intuition are aspects.

Then came the next great Teacher, the Christ. He embodied in Himself a still greater divine principle— greater than the Mind, that of Love; yet at the same time, He embraced within Himself all that the Buddha had of light. Christ was the expression of both light and love. Christ also brought to human attention three deeply necessary concepts:

1. The extreme value of the individual son of God and the necessity for intense spiritual effort.

2. The opportunity, presented to humanity, to take a great step forward and undergo the new birth.

3. The method whereby a man could enter into the kingdom of God, voiced for us in His words, "Love your neighbor as yourself". Individual effort, group opportunity and identification with each other—such is the message of the Christ.

Thus we have had four great Approaches of the divine to the human—two major Approaches and two lesser Approaches. These lesser Approaches made clear to us the true nature of the great Approaches and showed us how that which was conferred in the far distant history of the race constitutes a divine heritage and the seed of ultimate perfection.

A fifth great Approach is now possible and will take place when humanity has put its house in order. A new revelation is hovering over mankind and for it the previous four Approaches have prepared humanity. A new heaven and a new earth are on their way. The words "a new Heaven" signify an entirely new conception as to the world of spiritual realities and perhaps of the very nature of God Himself. May it not be possible that our present ideas of God as the Universal Mind, as Love and as Will may be enriched by some new idea and quality for which we have as yet no name or word and of which we have not the faintest understanding? Each of the three concepts as to the nature of divinity—mind, love and will—were entirely new when first presented to humanity.

What this fifth Approach will bring to humanity we do not and cannot know. It will surely bring as definite results in the human consciousness as did the earlier Approaches. For some years now, the spiritual Hierarchy of our planet has been drawing nearer to humanity and its approach is responsible for the great concepts of freedom which are so close to the hearts of men everywhere. The dream of brotherhood, of fellowship, of world cooperation and of a peace, based on right human relations, is becoming clearer in our minds. We are also visioning a new and vital world religion, a universal faith which will have its roots in the past, but which will make clear the new dawning beauty and the coming vital revelation.

Of one thing we can be sure, this fifth Approach will in some way—deeply spiritual, yet wholly factual— prove the truth of the immanence of God and will prove also the close relationship between God transcendent and God immanent, for both expressions of God are true.

IV. THE REGENERATION OF THE CHURCHES

Can the churches, both in the East and in the West, be regenerated, purified and brought into line with divine truth? Can they in reality take over the task which they loudly proclaim is theirs and become the genuine dispensers of truth and the representatives of the kingdom of God on earth? *The answer is yes.* These changes can be made and their possibility can be demonstrated by the recognition of certain factors which are oft overlooked.

A profound and sound optimism is entirely possible even in the midst of discouraging conditions. The heart of humanity is sound; God in His very nature and with all His power is present in the person of every man, unrevealed as yet in the majority but eternally present and moving towards full expression. Nothing can or ever has prevented mankind from a steady progress which has been from ignorance to knowledge and from darkness to light. The first great clause of the most ancient prayer in the world, "Lead us from darkness to Light", has seen fulfillment to a large degree. Today we are on the verge of seeing the answer to the second clause: "Lead us from the unreal to the Real". This may well be the outstanding effect of the coming fifth Approach.

God is not as He has been presented; salvation is not achieved as the churches teach; man is not the miserable sinner which the clergy force him to believe. All this is unreal but the Real exists; it exists for the churches and for the professional representatives of organized religion as much as for any other man or group. *Churchmen are as basically divine, as sound and as surely on their way to enlightenment as any other group of men on earth.* The salvation of the churches rests on the humanity of its representatives and on their innate divinity as surely as does the salvation of the mass of men. This is for the church a hard saying.

Great and good, holy and humble men are to be found serving as priests in every church, silently and quietly endeavoring to live as Christ would have them live, setting an example of a Christlike consciousness and demonstrating their close and recognized relation to God.

Let these men rise up, and in their spiritual might let them eliminate out of the churches those materially minded and narrow doctrinaires who keep the church as it is today; let them intensify the fire in their hearts and draw closer—with deliberation and understanding—to the Christ they serve; let them gather closer to the Hierarchy those they are seeking to help; let them discard—without fighting, comment or fury—the doctrines which hold the people in a mental prison and present those few and true teachings to which the hearts of all men everywhere respond. Let them have courage and cheer, optimism and joy, for the forces of evil have been greatly weakened and the masses of men are rapidly awakening to the true spiritual values; let them know that Christ and the true inner church are on their side; therefore, victory is already theirs.

The processes of evolution may be long but they are proven and sure and nothing can arrest the moving forward into the Kingdom of God. Humanity must progress; stage by stage and cycle after cycle, humanity approaches closer to divinity, discovers a more brilliant light and arrives at a growing knowledge of God. God, in the person of Christ and of His disciples, also draws nearer to men. What has been in the past shall indeed be in the future; revelation will succeed revelation until the great Informing Life of our planet (called in the Bible the Ancient of Days) will stand finally revealed in all His glory; He will then Himself approach His regenerated and purified people.

Another point which should be remembered is that in the new generation lies hope—hope through repudiation of the ancient and undesirable, hope because of their ceaseless demand for spiritual light, hope because of the promptness with which they recognize truth wherever it is to be found (in the church or out of it) and hope because, having been born in the midst of a ruined world and a general chaos, they are ready for the rebuilding.

The church will then proclaim that men can draw near to God, not through the mediation, absolution and the intercessory work of any priest or churchman but by right of man's inherent divinity. This it will be the duty of every churchman to evoke by example, by the energy of applied and practical love (not expressed through a soporific paternalism), and by the unified effort of the clergy of all faiths everywhere in the world.

The churches in the West need to realize that basically there is only one church but it is not necessarily only the orthodox Christian institution; God works in many ways, through many faiths and religious agencies; in their union will the fullness of truth be revealed. This is one reason for the elimination of nonessential doctrines.

V. THE NEW WORLD RELIGION

In what way will this new presentation of religion and its new rituals and ceremonies take form? A new presentation is deeply desired and hopefully anticipated by those to whom the religious attitude is of fundamental importance. What are the signs of its coming? What must be the preliminary first steps? Are there any indications of developing trends which would incline one to believe in its eventual appearance?

Many such questions arise. Much of what might be said in reply can be regarded by the skeptical and the orthodox as purely speculative. The present attitude of the churches would seem to negate any possibility of a universal religion at this time—if ever; the divergences in doctrine and in the presented approach to God would appear to preclude any uniformity of approach. Necessarily, the outer structure of the New World Religion will be long in manifesting; there is little chance of its full emergence during the present generation. The signs, however, of its rising are already to be seen on the horizon, and the dawn of true thinking is revealing them; the blueprints are already drawn. The inner attitude of humanity and a few outer happenings indicate a true inner recognition of the necessity for a revisal of orthodox religion and a revival of its spiritual influence. These are ever the preliminary steps to creation. Subjective realization always precedes the objective manifestation and so it is today in this case.

Humanity is recognizing the need for a more vital approach to God and one more intelligently presented; men are tired of doctrinal and dogmatic differences and quarrels; the study of Comparative Religion has demonstrated that the foundational truths in every faith are identical. Because of this universality, they evoke recognition and response from all men everywhere. The only factor in reality which militates against the spiritual unity of all men everywhere is the existent clerical organizations and their militant attitude to religions and to faiths other than their own.

In spite of all this, the structure of the New World Religion is being raised by the dissenting groups within the institutional churches, by the many world groups who present the concept of God immanent, even when they do so with selfish motive and with an unwholesome emphasis upon the powers of the indwelling divinity to provide perfect health, plenty of money, serene business success and unbroken popularity!

The New World Religion is also being brought into expression through the work of the esoteric groups throughout the world because of their particular emphasis upon the fact of the spiritual Hierarchy, upon the office and the work of the Christ and upon the techniques of meditation whereby soul-awareness (or the Christ-consciousness) can be achieved. Prayer has been expanded into meditation; desire has been lifted into mental aspiration. This is supplanted by a sense of unity and by the recognition of God immanent. This leads eventually to at-one-ment with God transcendent.

It is at this point that the Science of Invocation and Evocation can at times supersede the earlier techniques. The whole of humanity is moving forward into the area of mental understanding. The grasping nature of the prayers of the average men (based as they are upon desire for something) has long disturbed the intelligent; the vagueness of the meditation, taught and practised in the East and in the West (with its emphatically selfish note, personal liberation and personal satisfaction) is likewise causing a revolt. Something bigger and larger than individual desire and liberation is registered. Many groups are wrestling with these changes and this is, in itself, most hopeful.

In the aggregate of these groups—within the churches or outside them—is to be found the nucleus of the New World Religion. To this should be added the activities of the spiritualistic movement, not from the angle of its emphasis upon phenomena (much of it is spurious or imaginative, but some of it realistic and true) but from the angle of its surety about human immortality and the evidence which it has collected. The spiritualists have not yet succeeded in proving immortality; they have succeeded in proving survival and have thus made a valuable contribution to the structure of the New World Religion.

The slowly developing powers of telepathic communication and the recognition of extra-sensory perception by science are also playing their part in demonstration of the world of non-tangible life and values; all these factors necessitate and "sub-stand" the demand for a new presentation of religion which will be inclusive in its scope and not exclusive—as it is today. The religion of the future will account for the progress of humanity by its recognition of a divine Plan, historically proved. Scientifically applied discipline and training will enable mankind to function under the control of the inner divinity, or interior spiritual man; this training will also reveal to them the *fact* of God immanent in all forms and will enable them to participate in that great planetary movement—now slowly taking place—whereby God immanent is entering into a closer relation with God transcendent, via the spiritual Hierarchy of the earth.

The keynote of the New World Religion is *Divine Approach.* "Draw near to Him and He will draw near to you" is the injunction, emanating in new and clear tones from the Hierarchy today. *The great theme* of the New World Religion will be the unifying of the great divine Approaches; *the task* ahead of the churches is to prepare humanity, through organized and spiritual movements, for the fifth imminent Approach; *the method* employed will be the scientific and intelligent use of Invocation and Evocation and the recognition of its stupendous potency; *the objective* of the coming Approach, of the preparatory work and of the invocation, is revelation—a revelation which has ever been cyclically given and which today is ready for man's acceptance.

Invocation is of three kinds. There is, first of all, the massed demand, unconsciously voiced, and the crying appeal, wrung from the hearts of men in all times of crisis, such as the present. This invocative cry rises ceaselessly from all men living in the midst of disaster and is addressed to that power outside themselves which they feel can and should come to their help in their moment of extremity. That great and wordless invocation is rising everywhere today. Then there is the invocational spirit, evidenced by sincere men as they participate in the rites of their religion and take advantage of the opportunity of united worship and prayer to lay their demands for help before God. This group, added to the mass of men, creates a huge body of invocative applicants and, at this time, their massed intent is in great evidence and their invocation is rising to the Most High. Then, lastly, there are the trained disciples and aspirants of the world who use certain forms of words, certain carefully defined invocations and who—as they do— focus the invocative cry and the invocative appeal of the other two groups, giving it right direction and power. All these three groups are, consciously or unconsciously, swinging into activity at this time and their united effort guarantees a resultant evocation.

This new invocative work will be the keynote of the coming world religion and will fall into two parts. There will be the invocative work of the masses of the people, everywhere trained by the spiritually minded people of the world (working in the churches whenever possible under an enlightened clergy) to accept the fact of the approaching spiritual energies, focussed through Christ and His spiritual Hierarchy, and trained also to voice their demand for light, liberation and understanding. There will also be the skilled work of invocation as practised by those who have trained their minds through right meditation, who know the potency of formulas, mantrams and invocations and who work consciously. They will increasingly use certain great formulas of words which will later be given to the race, just as the Lord's Prayer was given by the Christ, and the New Invocation has been given out for use at this time by the Hierarchy.

This new religious science for which prayer, meditation and ritual have prepared humanity will train its people to present—at stated periods throughout the year—the voiced demand of the people of the world for relationship with God and for a closer spiritual relation to each other. This work, when rightly carried forward, will evoke response from the waiting Hierarchy and from its Head, the Christ. Through this response, the belief of the masses will gradually be changed into the conviction of the knowers. In this way the mass of men will be transformed and spiritualized, and the two great divine centers of energy or groups—the Hierarchy and Humanity itself—will begin to work in complete at-one-ment and unity. Then the Kingdom of God will in deed and in truth be functioning on earth.

It will be obvious to you that this technique of in-vocation and evocation has its roots in past methods of human approach to Deity. Men have long used the method of prayer with important and deeply spiritual results, in spite of its frequent misuse for selfish purposes; people, more intelligent and more mentally focussed, have employed more generally the method of meditation in order to arrive at knowledge of God, to awaken the intuition and to understand the nature of truth. These two methods of prayer and of meditation have brought humanity to the various spiritual recognitions which distinguish human thinking; through their means also the Scriptures of the world have been produced and the great spiritual concepts which have conditioned human living and which have led man on from one revelation to another have found their way into the minds of men. Worship also has played its part and has attempted to organize groups of believers into an oriented and united approach to God; however, the emphasis has again been on God transcendent and not on God immanent. When the God immanent in every human heart is awakened and functioning (even if only in a small degree) the potency of worship as an act of invocative approach to God will prove amazing and miraculous in its results. A response beyond man's deepest hopes will be evoked from Christ and His group of workers.

To these two great concepts underlying the New World Religion—Approach to God, and Invocation and

Evocation—must be added the exceedingly modern one of *energy* as the basis of all life, all forms and all action and the medium of all relationships. The force of the mind in producing telepathic rapport has already been recognized by science; mental power is today registered as an energy, capable of contact, of recognition and of producing a reciprocal activity.   Prayer has always recognized this, without attempting to formulate the mode whereby phenomena are produced through the medium of prayer. But in prayer, meditation and worship there is undoubtedly an energy factor, proceeding from *this* to *that* and producing in many cases the desired response in some form or another. Meditation is also an energy, setting in motion potencies which can eliminate certain aspects of thought or attract other aspects, such as visions, ideas, and spiritual recognitions. Worship has ever been known to produce a group stimulation when successfully oriented and focussed even to the point of ecstasy or hysteria, Pentecost or revelation. To these three—Prayer, Meditation and Worship—must now be added conscious Invocation, plus a trained expectancy of a reciprocal Evocation.

There are also many forms of energy and many spiritual potencies which are not as yet generally recognized but to which the church Festivals of all religions bear witness; these are released at the period of the Festivals. It is not possible in this book to deal with this subject in any detail.   But we can indicate the general line of thought which will produce and condition the New World Religion, which will link it with all of the good which the past has given, which will make it spiritually effective in the future and which today will slowly condition man's approach to God—an approach which for the first time in history can be organized on a worldwide scale and consciously undertaken. This indicates that because of man's desperate need, because of the crisis through which humanity has just passed and is now passing, men and women of vision and of inclusive thinking in all the churches of every world faith will end their doctrinal differences, agree on the essential religious truths and then proceed unitedly and with some uniformity of ritual and ceremonial to approach *together* the center of spiritual power.

Is this too much to expect and to ask of humanity in the hour of man's need? Cannot the enlightened members of the present great world religions in the East and in the West get together and plan for such an invocative undertaking and thus *together* inaugurate the mode of spiritual Approach which will serve to unify their efforts and establish the seed at least of the New World Religion?

The establishing of a measure of uniformity of procedure will not prove so difficult once a measure of unity on the spiritual essentials has been achieved. This carefully determined uniformity will aid men everywhere to strengthen each other's work and enhance powerfully the stream of thought energy which can be directed towards those spiritual Lives, working under the Christ, Who stand expectantly waiting to come to the aid of humanity. At present the Christian religion has its great Festivals; the Buddhist keeps his particular set of spiritual events, and the Hindu has still another list of holy days, as has also the Mohammedan. Is it not possible that in the world of the future, men everywhere and of all faiths will keep the same holy days and unite in honour of the same Festivals? This will bring about a pooling of spiritual resources and a united spiritual effort, plus a simultaneous spiritual invocation. The potency of this is surely apparent.

Let us indicate the possibilities of such a spiritual happening, and prophesy the nature of certain of the future worldwide Festivals. There are three such Festivals each year which all men could and would normally and easily keep together, in unison and with a uniformity of approach which would link them all closely together. These three Festivals are concentrated in three consecutive months and lead, therefore, to a prolonged annual spiritual effort which should affect the entire year. They would serve to unite in closer spiritual ties the Eastern and the Western believer; they express divinity in manifestation through the place where the will of God is known, through the spiritual Hierarchy where the love of God is fully expressed and through humanity whose task it is intelligently to work out God's plan in love and goodwill to all men.

I. *The Festival of Easter.* This is the festival of the risen, living Christ, the Head of the spiritual Hierarchy, the Inaugurator of the Kingdom of God and the Expression of the love of God. On this day, the spiritual Hierarchy which He guides and directs will be universally recognized, man's relation to it emphasized and the nature of God's love registered. Men everywhere will invoke that love, with its power to produce resurrection and spiritual livingness. This Festival is determined always by the date of the first Full Moon of spring. The eyes and thoughts of men will be fixed on life, not death; Good Friday will no longer be a factor in the life of the churches. Easter will be the great Western festival.

II. *The Festival of Wesak or Vaisakha.* This is the festival of the Buddha, that great spiritual Intermediary between the center where the will of God is known and the spiritual Hierarchy. The Buddha is the expression of the will of God, the embodiment of Light and the indicator of the divine purpose. Men everywhere will evoke wisdom and understanding and the inflow of light into the minds of men everywhere. This Festival is determined in relation to the Full Moon of Taurus.

It is the great Eastern festival and is already meeting with Western recognition; thousands of Christians today keep the festival of the Buddha.

III. *The Festival of Humanity.* This will be the festival of the spirit of humanity—aspiring to approach nearer to God, seeking conformity to the divine will to which the Buddha called attention, dedicated to the expression of goodwill which is the lowest aspect of love to which Christ called attention and of which He was the perfect expression. It will be the day pre-eminently on which the divine nature of man will be recognized and his power to express goodwill and to establish right human relations (because of his divinity) will be stressed. On this festival we are told Christ has for nearly two thousand years represented humanity and has stood before the Hierarchy as the God-man, the leader of His people and "the Eldest in a great family of brothers". This will, therefore, be a festival of deep invocation and appeal; it will express a basic aspiration towards fellowship and for human and spiritual unity; it will represent the effect in the human consciousness of the work of the Buddha and of the Christ. It will be held at the time of the Full Moon of Gemini.

If in these early days of restoration and of the inauguration of the new civilization and of the new world, men of all faiths and all religions, of every cult and all esoteric groups were to keep these three great Festivals of Invocation, simultaneously and with understanding of the far-reaching implications, a great spiritual unity would be achieved; if they unitedly invoked the spiritual Hierarchy and sought consciously to contact its Head a great and general inflow of spiritual light and love would occur; if they together determined, with steadfastness and understanding, to approach nearer to God, who could doubt the stupendous results which eventually would be seen? Not only would an underlying unity between men of all faiths be attained, not only would brotherhood be recognized as a fact and not only would our oneness of origin, of goal and of life be recognized but that which would be evoked would change all aspects of human living, would condition our civilization, change our mode of life and make the spiritual world a dominant reality in the human consciousness.

God, in the person of Christ and His Hierarchy would draw nearer to His people; God, through the instrumentality of the Buddha, would reveal His eternal light and evoke our intelligent cooperation; God, through the spiritual Hierarchy and through that center where the will of God is known, would bring humanity to the point of resurrection and to a spiritual awareness which would bring about goodwill towards men and peace on earth. The will of God transcendent would be carried out through the medium of God immanent in man; it would be expressed in love in response to the work of Christ; it would be intelligently presented on earth because the minds of men would have been illumined as the result of their united invocation, the unity of their effort and the oneness of their understanding.

It is for this that humanity waits; it is for this that the churches must work; it is these qualities and characteristics which will condition the New World Religion.

The great Invocation or Prayer does not belong to any person or group but to all Humanity. The beauty and the strength of this Invocation lies in its simplicity, and in its expression of certain central truths which all men, innately and normally, accept—the truth of the existence of a basic Intelligence to Whom we vaguely give the name of God; the truth that behind all outer seeming, the motivating power of the universe is Love; the truth that a great Individuality came to earth, called by Christians, the Christ, and embodied that love so that we could understand; the truth that both love and intelligence are effects of what is called the Will of God; and finally the self-evident truth that only through *humanity* itself can the Divine Plan work out.

THE GREAT INVOCATION

From the point of Light within the Mind of God
Let light stream forth into the minds of men.
Let Light descend on Earth.

From the point of Love within the Heart of God
Let love stream forth into the hearts of men.
May Christ return to Earth.

From the centre where the Will of God is known
Let purpose guide the little wills of men—
The purpose which the Masters know and serve.

From the centre which we call the race of men
Let the Plan of Love and Light work out
And may it seal the door where evil dwells.

Let Light and Love and Power restore the Plan on Earth.

CHAPTER VI

THE PROBLEM OF INTERNATIONAL UNITY

THE distribution of the world's resources and the settled unity of the peoples of the world are in reality one and the same thing, for behind all modern wars lies a fundamental economic problem. Solve that and wars will very largely cease. In considering, therefore, the preservation of peace, as sought for and emphasized by the United Nations at this time, it becomes immediately apparent that peace, security and world stability are primarily tied up with the economic problem. When there is freedom from want, one of the major causes of war will disappear. Where there is uneven distribution of the world's riches and where there is a situation in which some nations have or take everything and other nations lack the necessities of life, it is obvious that there is a trouble-breeding factor there and that something must be done. Therefore we should deal with world unity and peace primarily from the angle of the economic problem.

With the cessation of World War II came the opportunity to inaugurate a new and better way of life, and to establish that security and peace for which all men ceaselessly long. Three groups immediately appeared in the world:

1. The powerful, reactionary, conservative groups desirous of retaining as much of the past as possible, having great power and no vision.

2. The fanatical ideologists in every country—communistic, democratic and fascist.

3. The inert masses of the people in every land, ignorant for the most part, desiring only peace after storm and security in the place of economic disaster; they are victimized by their rulers, by established old conditions, and kept in the dark as to the truth of the world situation.

All these factors produce the present disorders and condition the deliberations of the United Nations. Though there is no major war, there is no peace, no security and no immediate hope of either.

It is essential for the future happiness and progress of humanity that there should be no return to the old ways, whether political, religious or economic. Therefore, in handling these problems, we should search out the wrong conditions which have brought humanity to its present state of almost cataclysmic disaster. These conditions were the result of religious faiths which have not moved forward in their thinking for hundreds of years; of economic systems which lay the emphasis upon the accumulation of riches and material possessions and which leave all the power and the produce of the earth in the hands of a relatively few men, while the rest of humanity struggle for a bare subsistence; and of political regimes run by the corrupt, the totalitarian-minded, the grafters and those who love place and power more than they love their fellowmen.

It is essential that there should be a presentation of these things in terms of *the spiritual welfare* of humanity and a truer interpretation of the meaning of the word "spiritual". The time is long past when a line of demarcation can be drawn between the religious world and the political or the economic. The reason for the corrupt politics and the greedy ambitious planning of so many of the world's leading men can be found in the fact that spiritually minded men and women have not assumed

—as their spiritual duty and responsibility—the leadership of the people. They have left the power in the wrong hands and permitted the selfish and the undesirable to lead.

The word "spiritual" does not belong to the churches or to the world religions. "Pure religion and undefiled" is pure charity and a selfless following of the Christ. The churches are themselves great capitalistic systems, particularly the Roman Catholic Church, and show little evidence of the mind that was in Christ. The churches have had their opportunity, but have done little to change men's hearts or to benefit the people. Now, under cyclic law, political ideologies and national and international planning are occupying the attention of the people and everywhere efforts are being made to bring about better human relations. This, in the eyes of the spiritually minded and of the enlightened worker for humanity, is a sign of progress and an indication of the innate divinity in man. That is truly spiritual which properly relates man to man and man to God and which demonstrates in a better world and the expression of the Four Freedoms throughout the planet. For these the spiritual man must work.

The Kingdom of God will inaugurate a world which will be one in which it will be realized that—politically speaking—humanity, as a whole, is of far greater importance than any one nation; it will be a new world order, built upon different principles to those in the past, and one in which men will carry the spiritual vision into their national governments, into their economic planning and into all measures taken to bring about security and right human relations. *Spirituality is essentially the establishing of right human relations,* the promotion of goodwill and finally the establishing of a true peace on earth, as the result of these two expressions of divinity.

The world today is full of warring voices; everywhere there is an outcry against world conditions; everything is being dragged out into the light of day; abuses are being shouted from the housetops, as the Christ prophesied they would be. The reason for all this outcry, discussion, and noisy criticism is that, as men awaken to the facts and begin to think and plan, they are aware of guilt within themselves; their consciences trouble them; they are conscious of the inequality of opportunity, of the grave abuses, of the entrenched distinctions between man and man, and the factor of racial and national discriminations; they question their own individual goals as well as national planning. The masses of men in every land are beginning to realize that they are largely responsible for what is wrong, and that their inertness and lack of right action and thinking has led to the present unhappy state of world affairs. This constitutes a challenge and no challenge is ever totally welcome.

The awakening of the masses and the determination of the reactionary forces and of the monied interests to preserve the old and fight the new are largely responsible for the present world crisis. The battle between the old, entrenched forces and the emerging, new idealism constitutes the problem today; other factors—though important, individually or nationally—are from the true and spiritual standpoint relatively negligible.

The unity, peace and security of the nations, great and small, are not to be attained by following the guidance of the greedy capitalist or the ambitious in any nation, and yet in many situations that guidance is being accepted. They are not to be gained by the blind following of any ideology, no matter how good it may seem to those conditioned by it; yet there are those who are seeking to impose their particular ideology on the world—and not solely in Russia. They will not be reached by sitting back and leaving the changing of conditions to God or the evolutionary process; yet there are those who make no move to help, even while knowing well the conditions with which the United Nations have to deal.

Unity, peace and security will come through the recognition—intelligently assessed—of the evils which have led to the present world situation, and then through the taking of those wise, compassionate and understanding steps which will lead to the establishing of right human relations, to the substitution of cooperation for the present competitive system, and by the education of the masses in every land as to the nature of true goodwill and its hitherto unused potency. This will mean the deflecting of untold millions of money into right educational systems, instead of their use by the forces of war and their conversion into armies, navies and armaments.

It is this that is spiritual; it is this that is of importance and it is this for which all men must struggle. The spiritual Hierarchy of the planet is primarily interested in finding the men who will work along these lines. It is primarily interested in humanity, realizing that the steps taken by humanity *in the immediate future* will condition the new age and determine man's destiny. Will it be a destiny of annihilation, of a planetary war, of worldwide famine and pestilence, of nation rising against nation and of the complete collapse of all that makes life worth living? All this can happen unless basic changes are made and made with goodwill and loving understanding. Then, on the other hand, we can have a period (difficult but helpful because educative) of adjustment, of concession and of relinquishment; we can have a period of right recognition of shared opportunity, of a united effort to bring about right human relations, and of an educational process which will train the youth of all nations to function *as world citizens* and not as nationalistic propagandists. What we need above all to see—as a result of spiritual maturity—is the abolition of those two principles which have wrought so much evil in the world and which are summed up in the two words: Sovereignty and Nationalism.

World Disunity

What at this moment appears to prevent world unity and keeps the United Nations from arriving at those necessary settlements which the man in the street is so eagerly awaiting? The answer is not hard to find and involves all nations: nationalism, capitalism, competition, blind stupid greed. It is an intense emotional nationalism which made the Polish nation so difficult a member of the family of nations; it is materialism and fear, plus a lack of spiritual interest, which makes France so constant an obstructionist and has led her to work against united world action; it is fanatical adherence to an ideology and national immaturity which prompts so much of Russia's activities; it is a rampant capitalism which makes the United States one of the most feared of the nations, plus her gestures of armed power; it is the fast dying imperialism which handicaps Great Britain and a clinging to responsibilities and territories which she is realizing could well be turned over to the United Nations; the hope of Great Britain lies in her socialistic tendencies which enable her to take the "middle path" between the communism of Russia and the capitalism of the United States. It is the smug greed of the nations which escaped the war which is hindering progress; it is the devious actions of the Jews and the hatred which they cultivate which tend also to undermine the hope of peace; it is the chaos in India and China which is complicating the work of the well-intentioned; it is the unchristian and undemocratic treatment of the Negro peoples in the United States and Africa which is con-

tributing to the ferment; it is the blind inertness and lack
of interest of the masses of the people which permit the
wrong men to be in power; it is fear of the rest of the
world which makes the Russian leaders keep their peoples
in ignorance of the attitude of other nations on world
affairs; it is the wrong use of money which colors the
press and the radio in Great Britain and still more in
the United States, thus keeping much of the truth from
the people; it is the upheaval of labor everywhere which
feeds the turmoil and forces unnecessary suffering upon
the public; it is powerful, political and international
distrust, lying propaganda and the apathy of the
churches which still further complicate the problem. It
is—above all else—the refusal of that public to face life
as it is and to recognize the facts for what they are. The
mass of men need arousing to see that good comes to
all men alike and not just to a few privileged groups,
and to learn also that "hatred ceases not by hatred but
that hatred ceases by love". This love is not a sentiment,
but practical goodwill, expressing itself through individuals, in communities and among nations.

Such is the sad and sorry picture of the world today
and only the blind and the uncaring will deny it. Only
a keen realization of the situation and of the sources of
the trouble will serve to impulse mankind to take the
needed action. But there is another side of the picture
and there is that which will balance the evil, though, as
yet, it will not completely balance and offset it.

Today men and women everywhere—in high place
and in low, in every nation, community and group—
are presenting a vision of right human relations which
must constitute the standard for the future of mankind.
Everywhere they are exposing the evils which must be
eliminated and they are educating ceaselessly in the
principles of the new age. It is these men who are of
importance. In politics there are great and wise states-

men who are endeavoring to guide their people wisely but have as yet too much with which to contend; of these Franklin D. Roosevelt was an outstanding modern example, for he gave of his best and died in the service of humanity. There are enlightened educators, writers and lecturers in every land who are seeking to show the people how *practical* is the ideal, how available the goodwill in mankind, and how easily applied are these ideals *when there are enough men and women of goodwill active in the world to force the issue.* This is the factor of importance. There are also scientists, physicians and agriculturists who have dedicated their lives to the betterment of human living; there are churchmen in all the faiths who follow sincerely the footsteps of the Christ (though they are not the leaders) and who repudiate the materialism which has ruined the churches; there are men and women in their untold millions who see truly, think clearly and work hard in their communities to establish right human relations.

Security, happiness and peaceful relations are desired by all. Until, however, the Great Powers, in collaboration with the little nations, have solved the economic problem and have realized that the resources of the earth belong to no one nation but to humanity as a whole, there will be no peace. *The oil of the world, the mineral wealth, the wheat, the sugar and the grains belong to all men everywhere.* They are essential to the daily living of the everyday man.

The true problem of the United Nations is a twofold one: it involves the right distribution of the world's resources so that there may be freedom from want, and it involves also the bringing about of a true equality of opportunity and of education for all men everywhere. The nations which have a wealth of resources are not owners; they are custodians of the world's riches and hold them in trust for their fellowmen. The time will inevitably come when—in the interest of peace and security—the capitalists in the various nations will be forced to realize this and will also be forced to substitute the principle of *sharing* for the ancient principle (which has hitherto governed them) of greedy grabbing.

There was a time—a hundred years or more ago—when a just distribution of the world's wealth would have been impossible. That is *not* true today. Statistics exist; computations have been made; investigation has penetrated into every field of the earth's resources and these investigations, computations and statistics have been published and are available to the public. The men in power in every nation know well exactly what food, minerals, oil and other necessities are available for worldwide use upon just and equitable lines. But these commodities are reserved by the nations involved as "talking and bargaining points". The problem of distribution is no longer difficult once the food of the world is freed from politics and from capitalism; it must also be remembered that the means of distribution by sea, rail and air are adequate.

None of this will, however, take place until the United Nations begin to talk in terms of humanity as a whole and not in terms of boundaries, of technical objectives and fears, in terms of the bargaining value of oil, as in the Near East, or in the language of mistrust and suspicion. Russia distrusts the capitalism of the United States and—to a lesser degree—that of Great Britain; South America is rapidly learning to mistrust the United States on the ground of imperialism; both Great Britain and the United States mistrust Russia, on the basis of her spoken word, her use of the veto and her ignorance of western idealism.

Yet it must be remembered that there are statesmen in Great Britain, the United States and Russia who are endeavoring to work for the common man and to speak on his behalf in the conclaves of the nations. As yet selfish opposition has rendered their work futile and the monied interests in many countries have negated their efforts. Russia has no monied interests, but she has vast resources in men and arms and these she plays off against the capitalistic interests. Thus the war goes on, and the man in the street waits hopelessly for a decision which will lead to peace—a peace based on security and right human relations.

To further complicate the problem, it must be borne in mind that the East and the West approach life from different angles. The Eastern approach is negative and subjective; the Western is positive and scientific and, therefore, objective. This is further complicated by the fact that western Europe and eastern Europe look at life and the modern problems from different angles; this makes cooperation difficult and definitely complicates the problems confronting the United Nations. Church and State are not in sympathy; capital and labor carry on a constant war; the man in the street pays the price and waits for justice and freedom.

World Unity

There is no counsel of perfection to give the world or any solution which will carry immediate relief. To the spiritual leaders of the race certain lines of action seem right and to guarantee constructive attitudes.

1. The United Nations, through its Assembly and Committees, *must* be supported; there is as yet no other organization to which man can hopefully look. Therefore, he must support the United Nations but, at the same time, let this group of world leaders know what is needed.

2. The general public in every nation *must* be educated in right human relations. Above all else, the children and the youth of the world must be taught

goodwill to all men everywhere, irrespective of race or creed.

3. Time must be given for the needed adjustments and humanity must learn to be intelligently patient; humanity must face with courage and optimism the slow process of building the new civilization.

4. An intelligent and cooperative public opinion must be developed in every land and the doing of this constitutes a major spiritual duty. This will take much time but *if* the men of goodwill and *if* the spiritual people of the world will become genuinely active, *it can be done in twenty-five years.*

5. The world economic council (or whatever body represents the resources of the world) *must* free itself from fraudulent politics, capitalistic influence and its devious scheming; it *must* set the resources of the earth free for the use of humanity. This will be a lengthy task but it will be possible when world need is better appreciated. An enlightened public opinion will make the decisions of the economic council practical and possible. Sharing and cooperation *must* be taught instead of greed and competition.

6. There must be freedom to travel everywhere in any direction and in any country; by means of this free intercourse, members of the human family may get to know each other and to appreciate each other; passports and visas should be discontinued because they are symbols of the great heresy of separateness.

7. The men of goodwill everywhere must be mobilized and set to work; it is upon their efforts that the future of humanity depends; they exist in their millions everywhere and—when organized and mobilized—represent a vast section of the thinking public.

It will be through the steady, consistent and organized work of the men of goodwill throughout the world that world unity will be brought about. At present, such men are only in process of organizing and are apt to feel that the work to be done is so stupendous and the forces arrayed against them are so great that their—at present—isolated efforts are useless to break down the barriers of greed and hate with which they are confronted. They realize that there is as yet no systemized spread of the principle of goodwill which holds the solution to the world problem; they have as yet no idea of the numerical strength of those who are thinking as they do. They ask themselves the same questions which are agitating the minds of men everywhere: How can order be restored? How can there be fair distribution of the world's resources? How can the Four Freedoms become factual and not just beautiful dreams? How can true religion be resurrected and the ways of true spiritual living govern the hearts of men? How can a true prosperity be established which will be the result of unity, peace and plenty?

There is only one true way and there are indications that it is a way towards which many millions of people are turning. *Unity and right human relations—individual, communal, national and international—can be brought about by the united action of the men and women of goodwill in every country.*

These men and women of goodwill must be found and organized and thus discover their numerical potency —for it is there. They must form a world group, standing for right human relations and educating the public in the nature and power of goodwill. They will thus create a world public opinion which will be so forceful and so outspoken on the side of human welfare that leaders, statesmen, politicians, businessmen and churchmen will be forced to listen and comply. Steadily and regularly, the general public must be taught an internationalism and a world unity which is based on simple goodwill and on cooperative interdependence.

This is no mystical or impractical program; it does not work through the processes of exposing, undermining or attack; it emphasizes the new politics, i.e., politics which are based upon the principle of bringing about right human relations. Between the exploited and the exploiting, the warmongers and the pacifists, the masses and the rulers, this group of men of goodwill will stand in their organized millions, taking no side, demonstrating no partisan spirit, fomenting no political or religious disturbance and feeding no hatreds. They will not be a negative body but a positive group, interpreting the meaning of right human relations, standing for the oneness of humanity and for practical, but not theoretical, brotherhood. The propagation of these ideas by all available means and the spread of the principle of goodwill will produce a powerful organized international group. Public opinion will be forced to recognize the potency of the movement; eventually the numerical strength of the men and women of goodwill in the world will be so great that they will influence world events. Their united voice will be heard on behalf of right human relations.

This movement is already gathering momentum. In many lands this plan for the formation of a group of people who are trained in goodwill and who possess clear insight into the principles which should govern human relations in world affairs is already past the blueprint stage. The nucleus for this work is present today. Their functions might be summarized as follows:

1. To restore world confidence by letting it be known how much goodwill—organized and unorganized —there is in the world today.

2. To educate the masses in the principles and the practice of goodwill. The word "goodwill" is largely

used at this time by all parties and groups, national and international.

3. To synthesize and coordinate into one functioning whole all the men and women of goodwill in the world who will recognize these principles as their *personal* directing ideal, and who will endeavor to apply them to current world or national events.

4. To create mailing lists in every country of the men and women of goodwill who can be counted upon to stand for world unity, right human relations and who will try—in their own lands—to reach others with this idea, through the medium of the press, the lecture platform and the radio. Eventually this world group should have its own newspaper or magazine, through means of which the educational process can be intensified and goodwill be found to be a universal principle and technique.

5. To provide in every country and eventually in every large city, a central bureau where information will be available concerning the activities of the men and women of goodwill all over the world; of those organizations, groups and parties who are also working along similar lines of international understanding and right human relations. Thus many will find those who will cooperate with them in their particular endeavor to promote world unity.

6. To work, as men and women of goodwill, with all groups who have a world programme which tends to heal world differences and national quarrels and to end racial distinctions. When such groups are found to work constructively and are free from scurrilous attack or aggressive modes of action, and actuated by goodwill to all men and are free from an aggressive nationalism and partisanship, then the cooperation of the men of goodwill can be offered and freely given.

It takes no great effort of the imagination to see that, if this work of spreading goodwill and educating public opinion in its potency is pursued, and if the men of goodwill can be discovered in all lands and organized, that (even in five years' time) much good can be accomplished. Thousands can be gathered into the ranks of the men of goodwill. This is the initial task. The power of such a group, backed by public opinion, will be tremendous. They can accomplish phenomenal results.

How to use the weight of that goodwill and how to employ the will to establish right human relations will grow gradually out of the work accomplished and meet the need of the world situation. The trained use of power on the side of goodwill and on behalf of right human relations will be demonstrated as possible, and the present unhappy state of world affairs can be changed. This will be done, not through the usual war-like measures of the past or the enforced will of some aggressive or wealthy group, but through the weight of a trained public opinion—an opinion which will be based on goodwill, on an intelligent understanding of the needs of humanity, on a determination to bring about right human relations and on the recognition that *the problems with which humanity is today confronted can be solved through goodwill.*

Training for new age
discipleship is provided
by the *Arcane School.*
The principles of the
Ageless Wisdom are
presented through esoteric
meditation, study and
service as a *way of life.*

*Write to the publishers
for information.*

INDEX

189

THE GREAT INVOCATION

From the point of Light within the Mind of God
Let light stream forth into the minds of men.
Let Light descend on Earth.

From the point of Love within the Heart of God
Let love stream forth into the hearts of men.
May Christ return to Earth.

From the centre where the Will of God is known
Let purpose guide the little wills of men —
The purpose which the Masters know and serve.

From the centre which we call the race of men
Let the Plan of Love and Light work out
And may it seal the door where evil dwells.

Let Light and Love and Power restore the Plan on Earth.

"The above Invocation or Prayer does not belong to any person
or group but to all Humanity. The beauty and the strength of this
Invocation lies in its simplicity, and in its expression of certain
central truths which all men, innately and normally, accept—the
truth of the existence of a basic Intelligence to Whom we vaguely
give the name of God; the truth that behind all outer seeming, the
motivating power of the universe is Love; the truth that a great
Individuality came to earth, called by Christians, the Christ, and
embodied that love so that we could understand; the truth that both
love and intelligence are effects of what is called the Will of God;
and finally the self-evident truth that only through *humanity* itself
can the Divine Plan work out."

ALICE A. BAILEY